Wonderful WORLD 3

PUPIL'S BOOK

Michele Crawford

T0349563

Contents

Unit	Reading	Vocabulary	Grammar
Introduction Hello! p 4-9		The Alphabet, Numbers, Days, Months, Dates, Seasons, Colours, The Body, Time, Classroom language	*a/an* Plurals *This/These – That/Those*
1 Family and Friends p 10-17	The Cortuga Mystery Emperor Penguins My Best Friend!	family members adjectives for people	*Be* Possessive Adjectives Possessive – *'s*
2 My Favourite Things p 18-25	The Cortuga Mystery The NG Kids' Shop What's your favourite thing?	toys possessions home entertainment	*Have got* *There is, There are* Prepositions of place
Review 1 p 26-27	Vocabulary and Grammar tasks / Song		
3 School Life p 28-35	The Cortuga Mystery Schools in Japan Anna's school	school subjects school equipment	Present Simple (aff, spelling) Present Simple (neg, question) Adverbs of Frequency
4 Hobbies p 36-43	The Cortuga Mystery Luna Park What do you do on Saturdays?	equipment for hobbies kinds of entertainment	Question words *Can* (ability, permission)
Review 2 p 44-45	Vocabulary and Grammar tasks / Song		
5 Celebrate! p 46-53	The Cortuga Mystery Carnival Crazy! Special Days around the World	parties fancy-dress costumes	Imperatives, Object pronouns, *Let's* Countable and uncountable nouns *Some/any*
6 Food! p 54-61	The Cortuga Mystery What can food tell us? Food around the World	food, drink and restaurant-related words	*Much/Many, How much …/many …* *A lot of/Lots of/A little/A few*
Review 3 p 62-63	Vocabulary and Grammar tasks / Song		
7 Sport p 64-71	The Cortuga Mystery Thai Boxing Ice Dancers	sports verbs of motion	Present Continuous (aff, spelling) Present Continuous (neg, question) Present Continuous (for the future)
8 People and Places p 72-79	The Cortuga Mystery Modern Cowboys Welcome to Scotland!	homes buildings jobs	Present Simple and Continuous *must*
Review 4 p 80-81	Vocabulary and Grammar tasks / Song		
9 Holidays and Travel p 82-89	The Cortuga Mystery Up, up and away! Cool Holidays!	means of transport holiday equipment	Past Simple of *be* Past Simple regular (aff, spelling) Past Simple irregular (aff)
10 Fame! p 90-97	The Cortuga Mystery Who was Walt Disney? Lessons in Fame	jobs in entertainment music films	Past Simple irregular (neg, question) *Wh …* questions in the Past Simple
Review 5 p 98-99	Vocabulary and Grammar tasks / Song		
11 Animals p 100-107	The Cortuga Mystery Presidents' Pets My clever pet!	wild and domestic animals adjectives to describe animals	Comparative Superlative Comparative and Superlative
12 Weather and Nature p 108-115	The Cortuga Mystery Nature in danger Looking for Tornados!	weather landscapes	*Be going to* Future Simple
Review 6 p 116-117	Vocabulary and Grammar tasks / Song		

National Geographic DVD Worksheets   p 118-123
Play   p 124-125
Irregular verbs   p 126

Listening	Speaking	Pronunciation	Functional language	Writing
Introduction of Cortuga Mystery characters Song	Dialogue introducing yourself		Introducing yourself	Personal fact file
Label pictures True or False Song	Talk about yourself	silent letters	Making friends	Punctuation Email
Multiple choice True or False Number correct order	Talk about favourite things Find differences between pictures	*the*	Playing games	Connectors *and* and *but* Advert
Blank filling Tick the correct school subjects Complete the table Song	Talk about everyday life	*oo* sounds	Talking about everyday life	Word order Description
Match Two-option lozenge Complete cinema information	Talk about your hobby Describe pictures	*w* sounds	Talking about hobbies	Verb forms Letter
Tick the correct box Match	Talk about special days	*s* and *sh* sounds	Making suggestions	Reference words Description
Tick the correct picture Tick or Cross things on a list Song Number pictures (recipe)	Talk about your favourite restaurant or café Dialogue	*ch* and *sh* sounds	Talking about food	Time words: order of events Recipe
Number the sports Write Yes or No Song	Describe the picture Talk about sports	*ea*, *ee* and *i* sounds	Talking about sport	Time expressions: word order Email
Complete the table Number jobs Multiple Choice	Talk about your home Find the differences between two pictures	Complete a poem (rhyming words)	Talking about places	Connectors: *because* and *so* Description
Tick the correct picture Number the places Song	Talk about your last holiday	*-ed* in Past Simple	Talking about travel	Adjectives Postcard
Multiple Choice Tick the correct film Complete the table	Play 'Guess the star' Practise a dialogue	*c, g, s, y* sounds	Talking about favourite stars	Paragraphs Review
Complete the table True or False Song	Compare these animals	*a* and *u* sounds	Talking about animals	Spelling Advert
Number the pictures Complete the table Number the pictures	Talk about your plans for the weekend Make predictions	*a* sounds	Talking about the weather	Checking for mistakes Letter

Introduction

These are scarlet macaw birds.
They are from South America.

Hello!

**Write. Then practise the dialogue
with your partner.**

> Hi!   I'm fine, thanks.
> My name's Polly.   I'm thirteen.

Max: Hello!

Polly: (1) _____

Max: What's your name?

Polly: (2) _____

Max: How are you?

Polly: (3) _____

Max: How old are you?

Polly: (4) _____

The Alphabet

A Write the missing letters. Then put them in the right order to make the name of this animal.

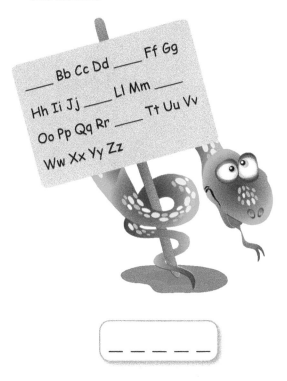

___ Bb Cc Dd ___ Ff Gg
Hh Ii Jj ___ Ll Mm ___
Oo Pp Qq Rr ___ Tt Uu Vv
Ww Xx Yy Zz

_ _ _ _ _ _

B 🎧 Listen and write the words.

1 _____   4 _____
2 _____   5 _____
3 _____   6 _____

Numbers

A Do the sums and write the answers.

	number	word
1 3 + 1 =	_____	_____
2 2 + 6 =	_____	_____
3 4 × 3 =	_____	_____
4 17 − 2 =	_____	_____
5 5 + 4 =	_____	_____
6 20 + 13 =	_____	_____
7 15 + 4 =	_____	_____
8 10 × 2 =	_____	_____
9 20 + 20 =	_____	_____
10 50 + 50 =	_____	_____

B Write the numbers and words.

	number	word
1 How old are you?	_____	_____
2 What number is your house?	_____	_____
3 How many kilos are you?	_____	_____

Days of the week

Put the days in the correct order. What's the missing day? Write it in the correct space.

Friday   Monday   Saturday   Sunday   Thursday   Wednesday

1 _____   5 _____
2 _____   6 _____
3 _____   7 _____
4 _____

Months

A Write the missing letters.

Janu __ ry   __ uly
Febr __ ary   A __ gust
Mar __ h   Septe __ ber
Apr __ l   Oc __ ober
Ma __   No __ ember
Ju __ e   De __ ember

B What's your favourite month?

_____

5

Dates

A Complete the dates in the diary, then read them.

June

1	Sunday	1 st
2	Tuesday	2 ___
3	Wednesday	3 ___
4	Thursday	4 ___
5	Friday	5 ___
6	Saturday	6 ___
7	Monday	7 ___

B Write these numbers in words.

1 12th _____

2 17th _____

3 21st _____

4 30th _____

5 9th _____

6 22nd _____

C Write these dates.

1 your birthday

_____

2 today's date

_____

3 on Tuesday

_____

4 the first day of the school year

_____

5 Christmas Day

_____

Seasons

Put the letters in the correct order to make the four seasons and write them in the correct place below.

gripns   mumres   unatmu   rewnti

_____   _____

_____   _____

Colours

🎧 Listen and colour the picture of Planet Od.

The Body

Match.

1	arm	☐	7	hand ☐
2	ear	☐	8	head ☐
3	eye	☐	9	leg ☐
4	finger	☐	10	mouth ☐
5	foot	☐	11	nose ☐
6	hair	☐	12	toe ☐

Telling the time

Complete the times with these words.

o'clock past quarter quarter to twenty-five

1 It's half _____ two.

2 It's one _____ .

3 It's _____ past eight.

4 It's ten _____ twelve.

5 It's _____ past nine.

6 It's _____ to five.

Classroom Language

Match the words and phrases with the pictures.

a Here you are.

b How do you spell ...?

c I don't know.

d Open your books ... .

e please

f Thank you

g What does ... mean?

Can I use your ruler, (1) _____ .

(2) _____ .

(3) _____ .

(4) _____ apple?

a–p–p–l–e

(5) _____ at page 26.

What's the answer to question 3?

(6) _____ .

(7) _____ flower _____ ?

a / an

Write a or an.

1 ____ dog
2 ____ girl
3 ____ egg
4 ____ hat
5 ____ ice cream

6 ____ pen
7 ____ orange
8 ____ animal
9 ____ mouse
10 ____ umbrella

Plurals

Write the plurals of these nouns in the correct columns.

> box   bus   child   family   foot
> glass   knife   mouse   tomato   toy

noun + s

book	books
(1) _____	_____

noun + es

watch	watches
(2) _____	_____
(3) _____	_____
(4) _____	_____
(5) _____	_____

noun + ies

country	countries
(6) _____	_____

noun + ves

life	lives
(7) _____	_____

irregular nouns

man	men
(8) _____	_____
(9) _____	_____
(10) _____	_____

This/These – That/Those

Look around you and talk about things using this, that, these and those. Use these words:

> bag   book   board   clock   desk   door   pen   pencil

This is a blue bag.   That's a brown bag.

These are pens.   Those are pencils.

Now complete the fact file about YOU!

Stick your photo here.

1 Name:
2 Age:
3 English class:
4 Favourite day of the week:
5 Favourite colour:
6 Hobbies:

Song

Cortuga Island. Beautiful island.
We're on Cortuga. You are. I am.
Hello, white sand. Hello, green sea.
We're on holiday. It's fun to be here.

Oo chooga chooga. We are on Cortuga.
Oo chooga chooga. Beautiful Cortuga.
Oo chooga chooga. We are on Cortuga now.

Cortuga Island. Mystery island.
This is Cortuga. Magic island.
We are here now. Robbie and Kate.
It's a happy holiday with Mandy and Jake.

1 Family and Friends

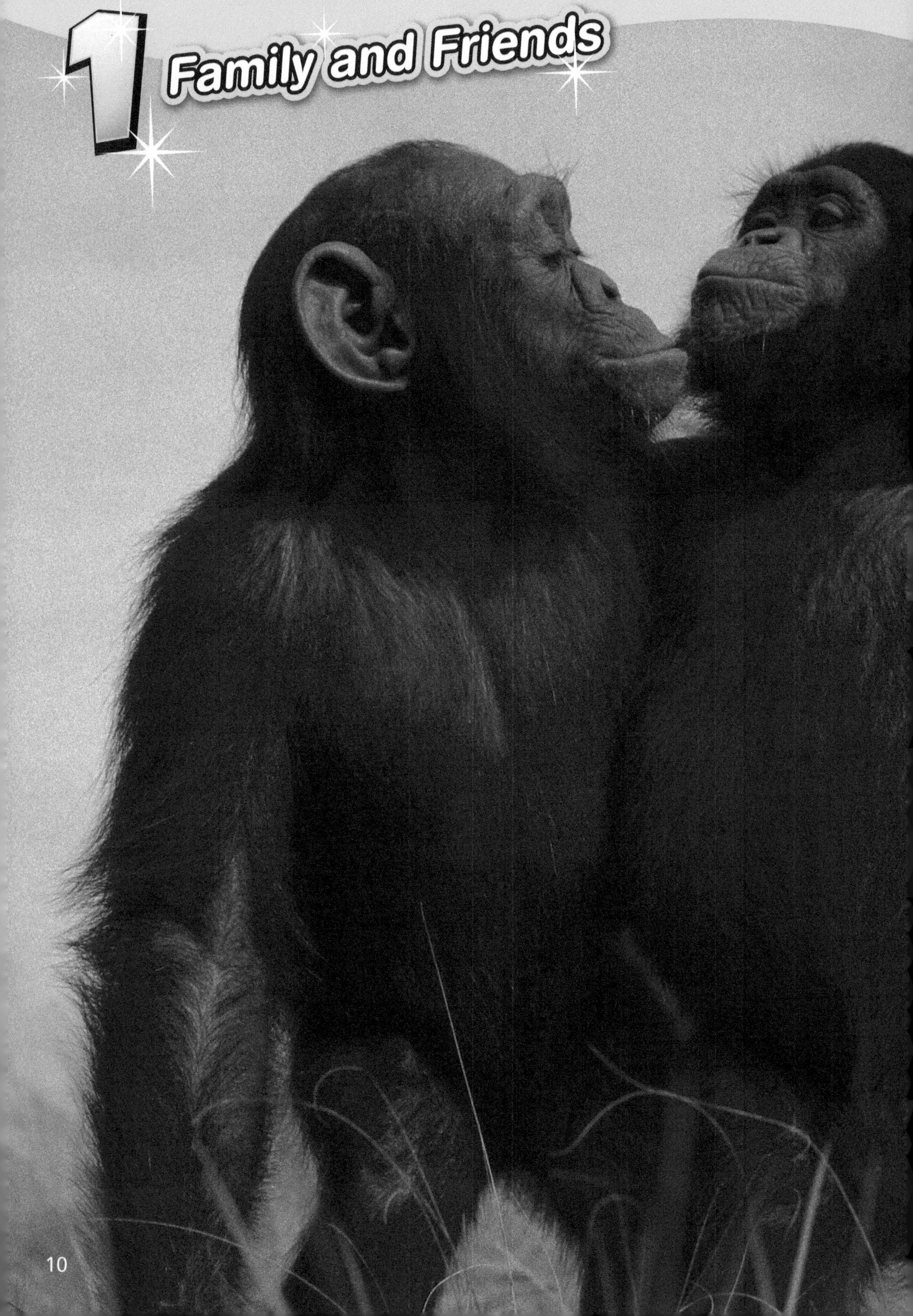

These are two young chimpanzees. They're great friends. They haven't got a mother or a father. They live in a special park in the Congo in Africa.

Quiz

Do you know the name of a very famous chimpanzee?

a   Jane
b   Tarzan
c   Cheeta

Lesson 1

🎧 **Listen and read.**

1

Jake! Jake! What's that?

Oh, no! It's a shark! Mandy! Get out of the water!

2
Robbie: Ha, ha! Hi, Kate!
Kate: Robbie! That's not funny!
Jake: What a stupid trick!

3
Jake: Hello. I'm Jake and this is my sister Mandy.
Mandy: Hi! This is cool!
Kate: Hi, I'm Kate and the 'shark' is my cousin Robbie.
Robbie: Hello and ... er, I'm sorry.
Jake: It's OK, Robbie.

4
Kate: We're on holiday here. What about you?
Jake: We're here for the summer holidays too. That's our uncle's house!
Kate: Wow! It's on the beach!
Mandy: There's Uncle Oliver. He's a scientist.
Robbie: Really? Kate's crazy about science.
Jake: Hi, Uncle Oliver! Meet our new friends, Kate and Robbie.
Oliver: Nice to meet you!

5

Please come for some lemonade this afternoon.

Good idea, Jake.

12

Vocabulary

A Complete the sentences with these words.

beach	friend	idea	scientist	shark

1 Mary's my _____ .

2 A _____ is a big fish.

3 It's a good _____ . You're cool!

4 A _____ is very clever.

5 We are at the _____ .

B Circle the correct words.

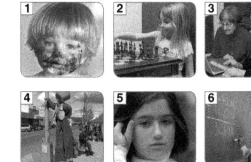

1 This is a baby with dark / fair hair.

2 Jenny's 5 years old and she's stupid / clever.

3 The man and woman are old / young.

4 He's tall / short and he's funny.

5 The girl is beautiful / ugly.

6 Here's a boy with black / grey hair.

Grammar

Be

We use be to talk about a person's:
a job.   *Uncle Oliver is a scientist.*
b nationality.   *We are English.*
c relatives.   *She is my sister.*
d name.   *I'm Mandy.*

Affirmative

I'm (I am)
you're (you are)
he's/she's/it's (he/she/it is)
we're/you're/they're (we/you/they are)

Negative	Question
I'm not (I am not)	Am I ...?
you aren't (are not)	Are you ...?
he/she/it isn't (is not)	Is he/she/it ...?
we/you/they aren't (are not)	Are we/you/they?

Short answers

Yes, I am.	No, I'm not.
Yes, he/she/it is.	No, he/she/it isn't.
Yes, you/we/they are.	No, you/we/they aren't.

A Complete the sentences with the correct form of be.

1 Kate and Robbie _____ cousins.

2 The trick _____ funny. It's stupid.

3 Tony and I _____ tall boys.

4 The house _____ old. It's new.

5 It's summer and we _____ on holiday.

6 Jake _____ a scientist. He's a pupil.

B Match.

1 Is Paul your cousin?   a Yes, it is.

2 Are the children in the house?   b No, she isn't.

3 Is the dog old?   c Yes, we are.

4 Are you eleven years old?   d Yes, I am.

5 Is she a tall girl?   e No, he isn't.

6 Boys, are you crazy about science?   f No, they aren't.

Listening

🎧 **Listen and write the names of Anna's friends.**

Becky	Jack	Jane	Rocky	Sam

Speaking

Ask and answer these questions with your partner.

Are you ten years old?   Is your dad/mum a scientist?
Am I your cousin?   Is your house new?
Are you funny?   What are you crazy about?

Writing

Write five sentences about one of your friends. Begin each sentence with He/She is ... or He/She isn't ... .

13

Lesson 2

Emperor Penguins

Reading

Read the article about a cool dad. Who is with the egg for two months?

Emperor penguins are amazing birds. They live in the Antarctic. They can't fly, but they are great swimmers. They're also good parents. The mother penguin has one egg every winter. She gives the egg to the father penguin and then she goes to the sea for food. Sometimes she walks about 80 kilometres! It's very cold in the Antarctic and the father penguin keeps the egg warm on his feet. He stays with the egg and he doesn't eat. Then after two months the chick (baby penguin) comes out of the egg. Soon the mother is back with food. The father penguin leaves. He goes back to the sea because he's very hungry.

Guess what!
About 40 kinds of birds can't fly.

Comprehension

Write T (true) or F (false).

1 Penguins are birds. ☐
2 Penguins can't swim. ☐
3 It isn't warm in the Antarctic. ☐
4 The mother penguin keeps her egg warm. ☐
5 The baby penguin goes to the sea. ☐

Vocabulary

Complete the sentences with these words.

| cold | egg | hungry | sea | warm |

1 It's _____ in winter.
2 Are you _____? Here's some food.
3 Penguins swim in the _____ .
4 Every winter a mother penguin has one _____ .
5 It isn't _____ in winter.

Grammar

Possessive adjectives show that something belongs to someone or something.
Dad is 37 years old. His name is Barry.

Subject Pronouns	Possessive Adjectives
I	my
you	your
he	his
she	her
it	its
we	our
you	your
they	their

Note: Be careful with these words:
• it's (it is) and its
• you're (you are) and your
• he's (he is) and his

Complete the sentences with the correct possessive adjectives.

1 Mum is 34 years old. _____ birthday is in May.
2 Look at that dog! _____ ears are big!
3 Nancy and Lee are good friends. _____ parents are friends too.
4 James is very tall but _____ brother is short.
5 We are sisters. _____ names are Kim and Kerry.
6 Hi, Jenny! Is this _____ cousin?
7 I'm Vicky and this is _____ friend, Sue.
8 You and Tom are tall and _____ hair is brown.

Vocabulary

Complete the pairs with these words.

| dad   daughter   grandad   sister   uncle   wife |

mum and _____

brother and _____

grandma and _____

husband and _____

aunt and _____

son and _____

Listening

🎧 **Listen to Ben talking about his aunt and uncle. Write T (true) or F (false).**

1 Uncle Peter is tall. ☐
2 Uncle Peter's eyes are dark. ☐
3 Aunt Jenny is thirty-five years old. ☐
4 Aunt Jenny isn't a scientist. ☐
5 Tina is Ben's daughter. ☐

🎧 **Sounds of English**

A Listen to these words. What do you notice about the red letters?

1 answer
2 scientist
3 what

B Now say these words. Circle the silent letters. Then listen and check your answers.

1 f r i e n d
2 l i s t e n
3 w h e r e
4 t w o

Song

I'm a chick. Chick! I'm a penguin chick.
You're a chick. Chick! You're a penguin chick.
We are Emperor penguins
And we go to the sea to eat.

And we walk, walk our penguin walk.
Yes, we walk, walk our funny walk.
I'm not cold in winter.
I'm warm on my father's feet.

My mother can't fly. My father can't fly.
Emperor penguins can't fly.
But we're great swimmers. We love the sea!
My penguin friends and my family.

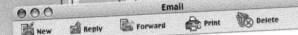

My Best Friend!

Email

New | Reply | Forward | Print | Delete

Hi!

I'm Errol and I'm 11 years old. I'm from England.

My best friends are Mike and Greg. They're twins and they're eleven years old. They're cool! The twins' hair is brown. We're together in Class 3A at school. Mike is very clever, and Greg is very funny. Our birthdays are on the same day – 8th February!

Who is your best friend?

Email me at: errol@epalengland.com

Email

New | Reply | Forward | Print | Delete

Hello!

I'm Lara and I'm French. I'm 9 years old.

Sophie is my best friend. She's 29 years old. Her hair is fair and her eyes are green. She's beautiful and she's my mum! Sometimes I do stupid things, but she says 'It's OK, it doesn't matter.'

Is your mum your best friend?

My email is: lara@fra.com

Comprehension

Answer the questions.

1 What class is Errol in?

_____

2 What are the twins' names?

_____

3 When is Errol's birthday?

_____

4 Where's Lara from?

_____

5 How old is Lara's mum?

_____

Say it like this!

Making friends

Ask and answer these questions with a partner.

What's your name?
My name's _____ .

How old are you?
I'm _____ years old.

Where are you from?
I'm from _____ .

When's your birthday?
My birthday's on (the) _____ (of) _____ .

Grammar

Possessive 's

We use 's after singular nouns and an apostrophe (') after plural nouns to show something belongs to someone.
This is Emma's dog.
Ron is the boys' dad.

Note: Plural irregular nouns (without s) are followed by 's.
The children's grandad is nice.

Write the apostrophe (') in the correct place.

1 Janes eyes are brown.

2 The babies names are Amy and Anthony.

3 Henrys tricks aren't funny.

4 The childrens uncle is a scientist.

5 Sheila is my mums best friend.

6 The womans name's Sarah.

Writing

Punctuation

A Match.

1	capital letter	a	**'**
2	full stop	b	**A**
3	question mark	c	**.**
4	apostrophe	d	**?**

B Write the sentences using the correct punctuation and the correct capital letters.

1 im dans sister

_____

2 are you Rachels friend

_____

3 penguins are amazing animals

_____

4 my dogs very clever

_____

5 its a great house

_____

C Read Florence's email. Find seven mistakes and correct them.

Hi!

I'm florence and i'm from france. I'm eleven years old i'm tall with dark hair and green eyes.

my sister Corinne is six years old and my brother jean is a baby.

I'm crazy about sport and my cat, Felix

What are you crazy about?

Email me at:
FlorenceRouen@fra.com

Task

D Write an email about yourself. Use this plan to help you.

Begin like this:
Hi!

Answer the questions:
What's your name?

_____

Where are you from?

_____

How old are you?

_____

What are your brothers' and sisters' names?

_____

How old are they?

_____

What are you crazy about?

_____

Finish like this:
Email me at _____
(your email address)

E Read your email and check capital letters, full stops, apostrophes and question marks.

2 My Favourite Things

Quiz

Look at the picture. What are the children playing with?

a balloons

b planes

c kites

2 Lesson 1

🎧 **Listen and read.**

1)
Jake:	Hello! Uncle Oliver?
Mandy:	He isn't here.
Robbie:	He's got some strange things! Look! A toy lizard!
Kate:	Yes, it's ... aaargh! It's REAL! Yuk!
Mandy:	That's Uncle Oliver's pet lizard, Henry.

2)

I've got a message on my mobile phone.

Who is it from?

It's from Uncle Oliver. 'Sorry! I'm at the museum. I've got lots of work.'

3)
Robbie:	This is a great laptop. Have you got any computer games?
Jake:	No, Robbie. I'm sorry, it's Uncle Oliver's laptop. Please don't touch it.

4)
Kate:	What's that, Mandy?
Mandy:	A puzzle!
Kate:	Look! There's a message on it. Find the pieces and then see the answer to the mystery.
Robbie:	Wow! A mystery!
Mandy:	But where are all the pieces?
Jake:	I don't know.

5)

Hey! What ....?

I'm scared!

Wow!

Vocabulary

A Circle the correct words.

1 Have you got computer pieces / games?
2 The museum has got lots of things / puzzles.
3 This animal isn't real – it's a toy / pet.
4 There's a new mystery / message on your mobile phone.
5 Lizards are scared / strange animals.

B Match.

1 skateboard ☐
2 laptop ☐
3 board game ☐
4 teddy bear ☐
5 robot ☐
6 bike ☐

Grammar

Have got

We use have got to:
a describe someone/something.
   I've got black hair.
b show that something belongs to someone/something.
   She's got a ball.

Affirmative

I've/you've/we've/they've (have) got
he's/she's/it's (has) got

Negative

I/you/we/they haven't (have not) got
he/she/it hasn't (has not) got

Question

Have I/you/we/they got ...?
Has he/she/it got ...?

Short answers

Yes, I/you/we/they have.   No, I/you/we/they haven't.
Yes, he/she/it has.   No, he/she/it hasn't.

Note: Be careful with its (possessive adjective) and
it's (it has) got.

A Complete the sentences with the correct form of have/has got.

My name's Liz. I (1) _____ (✔) a friend.
Her name's Sasha. She (2) _____ (✗) big
ears, but she (3) _____ (✔) big eyes. Sasha
(4) _____ (✗) brown eyes. Her eyes are
blue. I (5) _____ (✔) a brother but Sasha
(6) _____ (✗) a brother. Sasha
(7) _____ (✔) lots of toys, but she
(8) _____ (✗) a computer. We're great
friends. Who is Sasha? She's my cat!

B Write questions and answers.

1 Jake / a mobile phone?

   _____

   Yes, _____ .
2 Jake and Mandy / an aunt?

   _____

   No, _____ .
3 you / a pet lizard, Jamie?

   _____

   Yes, _____ .
4 your sister / a skateboard?

   _____

   No, _____ .

Listening

🎧 Listen and circle the correct answers.

1 Bruno is ____
   a Robin's friend.   b a teddy bear.
2 Who is very old?
   a Robin   b Bruno
3 Robin has got lots of ____
   a computer games.   b board games.
4 Robin and Vicky have got ____
   a computer games.   b skateboards.
5 Robin's favourite thing is ____
   a a bike.   b white and fast.

Speaking

Ask and answer these questions with your partner.

What's your favourite toy or game?
Have you got a laptop/skateboard/bike?
Has your family got a pet? What is it?
What's your friend's/Dad's/Mum's favourite thing?

Writing

**Write five sentences about the things you have got
and what your favourite thing is.**

Reading

Look at the website. Choose one thing you like and one thing you don't like. Say why.

The Kids' Shop

NATIONAL GEOGRAPHIC KIDS

Read about these exciting things. They're great presents for your family and friends!

1

Remote Controlled Tarantula
(ages: 6-8 years)

Is this a real spider?
No, it isn't! It's a toy and it's got eight moving legs.
It's big and scary!
Do you like tricks?
Then this is the toy for you.

3

Creepy Creatures DVD
(for all ages)

There are lots of strange animals from the real world on this DVD! You can see monsters like vampire bats and Komodo dragons (very big lizards)! It's a good present for your friends.

2

Interactive Talking Globe
(ages: 8-12 years)

This is a talking map of the world! There's a magic pen with the globe. Touch a country with the pen and the globe tells you about it! It's also a great help with homework.

4

Moon Shoes
(ages: 7+)

You can't go to the moon but you can walk on the moon. How? Wear these shoes! They're great fun. You can walk and feel like an astronaut. These shoes are for all the family, even your mum and dad.

Guess what!
Real tarantulas have got eight eyes, but they can't see well.

Comprehension

Write **SP** (Spider), **D** (DVD), **SH** (Shoes) or **G** (Globe).

1 There are strange animals on this. ☐
2 You can move in a strange way. ☐
3 This has got information about different places. ☐
4 This is good for tricks. ☐

Vocabulary

Complete the sentences with these words.

country	exciting	moving	present	scary

1 Spain is a big _____ .
2 The robot has got _____ arms and legs.
3 Computer games are fast and _____!
4 Here is your _____ . Happy Birthday!
5 Sharks are _____ animals!

Grammar

There is, There are

We use there is and there are to describe scenes and talk about place.
There is a girl in the shop.
There are some books on the desk.

Affirmative

There's (There is) a(n) ...
There are (some) ...

Negative

There isn't (is not) a(n) ...
There aren't (are not) (any) ...

Question

Is there a(n) ...?
Are there (any) ...?

Short answers

Yes, there is. / No, there isn't.
Yes, there are. / No, there aren't.

A Put the words in the correct order to make sentences.

1 aren't / maps / at / any / school / there

   _____

2 ? / in / a / there / your / is / robot / classroom

   _____

3 lots of / are / girls / in / class / there / our

   _____

4 ? / there / spiders / are / any / here

   _____

5 isn't / a / there / here / skateboard

   _____

B Answer the questions.

1 Are there any maps in your classroom?

   _____

2 Is there a spider in your classroom?

   _____

Prepositions of place

in   on   next to   near

under   between   in front of   behind

C Look at the picture and complete the sentences with prepositions of place.

1 The boy is _____ the desk.
2 The teddy bears are _____ the box.
3 The desk is _____ the door.
4 The map is _____ the girls.
5 The cat is _____ the bed.
6 The photos are _____ the computer.
7 The box is _____ the bed.
8 The bed is _____ the desk.

Vocabulary

Write the correct words.

camera   globe   ice skates
comic   piano   watch

_____

_____

Listening

🎧 **Listen to Helen and Oliver and write T (true) or F (false).**

1 Tom's birthday is on Friday.
2 Helen has got a present for Tom.
3 Books aren't Oliver's favourite things.
4 The shop near Helen's house has got computer games.
5 Tom hasn't got any DVDs.

23

Reading

Read the article and write the children's names under their photos.

_____

_____

What's your favourite thing?

Dan, 11

My friends are crazy about computer games, but I like books. My friends say books are boring. I love stories. *Lord of the Rings* is my favourite book.

Amy, 13

My favourite thing is my guitar. It's my mum's guitar really and it's fifteen years old! Mum doesn't play it now. I have lessons and I'm quite good. The lessons are difficult but they're fun.

_____

Tom, 12

My family and I have got a boat. Its name is 'Sea Queen' and it's red and white. It isn't very big but it's great! It's my favourite thing. Here's a photo of me, my mum, my dad and my sister on our boat.

Miranda, 7

My teddy bear, Candy, is my favourite thing. I have great fun with Candy. My baby brother, Tony, is crazy about Candy too but I say: 'Don't touch Candy. You've got toys too! Candy is my teddy bear!'

Comprehension

Write D (Dan), A (Amy), T (Tom) or M (Miranda). Who ...

1 has got a favourite toy? ☐
2 is different from his/her friends? ☐
3 has got a brother? ☐
4 has got something with two colours? ☐
5 has got something from their mum? ☐

Say it like this!

Playing games

Complete the dialogues with these phrases.

Can I have a go? Catch! It's my/your turn!
Slow down! Well done!

Bill: Great computer game! (1) _____
Jake: OK. Here you are.

Dad: Are you scared?
Sue: Yes, Dad. (2) _____

Ben: (3) _____
Jane: Oh! I'm sorry. You play now.

Kay: I've got 300 points!
Tina: That's very good. (4) _____

Jim: Here's the ball. (5) _____
Kate: OK, I'm ready!

Now practise the dialogues with your partner.

Listening

🎧 **Listen and number the children's things in the correct order.**

a skateboard ☐

b ball ☐

c computer game ☐

d board game ☐

Speaking

Find four differences between the two pictures. Use have/has got and there is/are.

1️⃣

2️⃣

🎧 **Sounds of English**

Listen and repeat. How do you say the word the in 1 and 2, and 3 and 4?

1 the computer   3 the animal

2 the toy   4 the uncle

Writing

Connectors

A Read about and and but.

We use and to add something else to a sentence.
Computers are exciting and fun.

We use but to show that something is very different from another thing.
The magazine is new but it's boring.

B Complete the sentences with and or but.

1 My watch is green _____ black.

2 This DVD is strange _____ it's cool.

3 Ben _____ Sam have got kites.

4 I've got a cat _____ a dog.

5 The camera is new _____ it isn't very good.

C Read this advert and circle the correct words.

Bike for sale!

It's blue (1) but / and it's beautiful.
It's a great bike. It isn't new
(2) but / and it's very fast.
It's great for a tall boy
(3) and / but not for a short boy.

Price: £60

Ring: 345 7533 (4) and / but ask for Harry.

Task ✏️

D Write an advert for one of your favourite things. Use this plan to help you.

Answer the questions

What is it?

_____

Is it new or old?

_____

What colour is it?

_____

Is it big, small, fast, beautiful, etc?

_____

Why is it great?

_____

E Remember to use and and but to join your ideas together.

Review 1

Vocabulary

A Find the stickers.

1	2
beautiful	hungry

3	4
old	scary

5	6
cold	warm

7	8
funny	young

B Complete the table.

aunt   board game   daughter   grandma   lizard
penguin   puzzle   shark   teddy bear

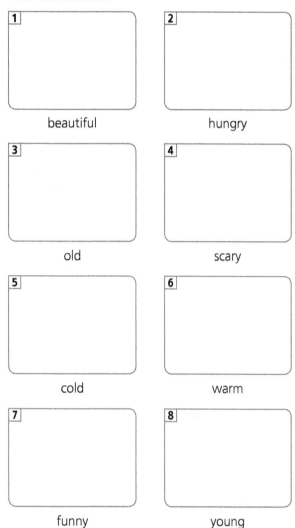

Family	Toys	Animals
_____	_____	_____
_____	_____	_____
_____	_____	_____

C Choose the correct reply.

1 Hi! I'm Danny.
  a I've got lots of work.
  b Nice to meet you!

2 Come to the beach this afternoon!
  a Good idea!
  b That's strange.

3 What's this?
  a Have fun!
  b I don't know.

4 I've got a new bike.
  a I'm sorry.
  b It's cool!

5 This computer is great!
  a Don't touch!
  b Don't go!

6 I'm sorry, Mum.
  a Well done!
  b It's OK. It doesn't matter.

Grammar

A Circle the correct answers.

1 Is / Am Chris your cousin?
2 We not are / are not friends.
3 Sharks isn't / aren't boring!
4 Am I / I am tall or short?
5 That lizard be / is real!
6 Are / Is you good at board games?

B The words in bold are wrong. Write the correct words.

1 This is my grandad.
   Her son is my dad.   _____

2 We are sisters. That's
   their house over there.   _____

3 My brother's toys are
   very old. **My** teddy bear
   has got one ear!   _____

4 John and Sam are lucky.
   His dad has got a boat!   _____

5 That's Emma's dog.
   Your name is Rex.   _____

6 I'm Benny. This is **his**
   skateboard!   _____

C Complete the sentences with the correct possessive form of the words in brackets.

1 His _____ bike is red and white. (dad)

2 The _____ toys are in the box. (babies)

3 The _____ faces have got big noses and long ears. (monsters)

4 The _____ skateboards are red and white. (children)

5 Who is _____ brother? (Polly)

6 This isn't their _____ house. (family)

D Complete the sentences with have/haven't got or has/hasn't got.

1 Kate _____ black hair. Her hair is fair.

2 A week _____ seven days.

3 Dogs _____ five legs.

4 September _____ thirty one days.

5 Your dad _____ a car, but he's got a bike.

6 Spiders _____ eight legs.

7 Penguins _____ two feet.

8 Uncle Oliver _____ a house on the beach.

E Write short answers.

1 Have you got fair hair?

_____

2 Has your dad got a guitar?

_____

3 Has your mum got blue eyes?

_____

4 Have your friends got any pets?

_____

5 Have you and your friends got any computer games?

_____

6 Has your house got lots of windows?

_____

Song

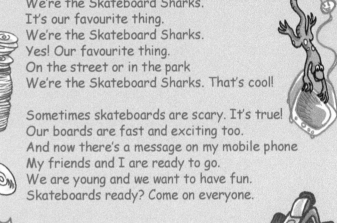

I've got games, a computer and a camera too.
My sister's got a lizard and new Moon Shoes.
We've got MP3s, DVDs and lots of CDs.
Sometimes it's boring to watch TV.
It's summer now and we want to get out.
And do the thing we're crazy about.

We're the Skateboard Sharks.
It's our favourite thing.
We're the Skateboard Sharks.
Yes! Our favourite thing.
On the street or in the park
We're the Skateboard Sharks. That's cool!

Sometimes skateboards are scary. It's true!
Our boards are fast and exciting too.
And now there's a message on my mobile phone
My friends and I are ready to go.
We are young and we want to have fun.
Skateboards ready? Come on everyone.

3 School Life

Quiz

What is the girl wearing?

a a party dress
b school uniform
c a pretty skirt

3 Lesson 1

🎧 **Listen and read.**

1
Jake:	Where are we?
Kate:	Hey! We're in a school.
Robbie:	What a cool mystery!
Mandy:	Oh, no! Look at the date! It's 1885!
Teacher:	Silence!

2
Teacher:	What's the answer to this sum?
Tom:	It's ... er ...
Jake:	It's 153.
Tom:	Er ... the answer is ... um ... 153, Miss.
Teacher:	Correct! Well done, Tom!

3 At break time ...
Robbie:	That teacher isn't very nice.
Tom:	Where are you from?
Jake:	Well ..., we're from the future.
Tom:	Amazing! And is that a magic machine?
Jake:	No, it isn't. It's just a calculator.
Tom:	Does it always give the correct answers?
Jake:	Yes. I use it all the time at my school.

4
Tom:	Please have this! I've got it for good luck.
Jake:	Wow! It's a piece of the puzzle! Thanks a lot! You keep the calculator, OK?

5 Bye, Tom!

Vocabulary

Write the missing letters.

1 6th April 2010 is one.

   d _ _ _

2 A question has got one.

   a _ _ _ _ _ _

3 1+1=2 is one.

   s _ _

4 He/She works in a school.

   t _ _ _ _ _ _ _

5 This is a machine for maths lessons.

   c _ _ _ _ _ _ _ _ _ _

Grammar

We use the Present Simple to talk about:
a general truths.
   Children go to school.
b things we do regularly.
   We play in the park every day.
c permanent states.
   Jan works in an English school.

Affirmative

I/you/we/they play
he/she/it plays

Spelling rules

I	he/she/it	
like	likes	
go	goes	
watch	watches	**Note:**
brush	brushes	I have but he/she/it has.
study	studies	
play	plays	

Time expressions

every day/night/week/month/year
at the weekends
in the morning/afternoon/evening
on Thursdays

Time expressions can go at the beginning or end
of a sentence.
At the weekends we play on the beach.
My friends and I go to the cinema every Saturday.

A Complete the table.

I	he/she/it
stay	(1) _____
wash	(2) _____
fix	(3) _____
carry	(4) _____
touch	(5) _____
give	(6) _____

B Complete the sentences with the Present Simple of the verbs in brackets.

1 We _____ (go) to school in the morning.
2 Karen _____ (like) her teacher.
3 I _____ (use) a calculator in the maths lessons.
4 On Saturdays you _____ (play) football at school.
5 My brother _____ (study) in the afternoon.
6 Tom _____ (have) fun at school every day.
7 Sue and her sister _____ (do) their homework every night.
8 In the evening Ron's cat _____ (sit) on his desk.

Vocabulary

Match.

1 English ☐
2 maths ☐
3 history ☐
4 geography ☐
5 science ☐
6 art ☐
7 music ☐
8 sport ☐

Listening

🎧 **Listen and write the school subjects.**

Lesson 1: _____   Lesson 3: _____

Lesson 2: _____   Lesson 4: _____

Speaking

Talk about school. Ask and answer these questions with your partner.

What class are you in?
What's your favourite subject?
Who's your favourite teacher?
How many children are there in your class?
What have you got in your school bag?

Writing

Write five sentences about your school. Answer the questions in the Speaking task.

Reading

Read about schools in Japan. Say what is different at your school.

Schools in Japan

Japanese pupils usually walk to school and they wear helmets. In some schools they also wear a uniform. Pupils start lessons at 8.30 am and they finish at 3.50 pm. They do subjects like Japanese, maths, history and English. They do lots of homework too.

Pupils have lunch at school. They usually eat in their classroom. Some pupils carry the food to the classroom from the cafeteria. These pupils wear special masks! Pupils don't only eat Japanese food. They also eat things like spaghetti or burgers. After lunch, pupils always brush their teeth. Then they clean their classroom!

What do Japanese pupils do after school? Well, there are a lot of clubs for pupils. They can choose a sports team, a musical club, an art club, or a science club. Shoko, an eleven year old from Tokyo, likes the karaoke club at her school. 'We sing songs and have fun there,' she says.

Guess what!
Japanese pupils don't wear shoes at school. They wear slippers!

Comprehension

Write T (true) or F (false).

1 Japanese pupils ride a bicycle to school. ☐
2 Japanese pupils never wear a school uniform. ☐
3 Japanese pupils have lunch at home. ☐
4 Pupils in Japan clean their classrooms. ☐
5 Shoko sings after school. ☐

Vocabulary

Circle the correct words.

1 Does he brush / clean his classroom?
2 The children sing / say songs in their music lessons.
3 What time do you finish / go school on Fridays?
4 We wear / carry uniforms at our school.
5 I have / do fun at my art club.
6 Pupils make / do lots of homework every day.

Grammar

Present Simple

Negative

I/you/we/they don't (do not) like
he/she/it doesn't (does not) like
We don't have lunch at school.

Question

Do I/you/we/they like ...?
Does he/she/it like ...?
Does your sister go to school?

Short answers

Yes, I/you/we/they do.   No, I/you/we/they don't.
Yes, he/she/it does.   No, he/she/it doesn't.
Does he like sports?   *No, he doesn't.*

Choose the correct answers.

1   I _____ history and maths lessons.
    a doesn't like   b don't like

2   _____ to school every day?
    a Do we go   b We go

3   Does Mandy walk to school? Yes, she _____ .
    a don't   b does

4   Jim _____ use a computer.
    a don't   b doesn't

5   _____ John and Sue have lunch at 12 o'clock?
    a Do   b Does

6   Does your dad go to school? No, _____ .
    a he doesn't   b he don't

7   Their teacher _____ wear jeans at school.
    a don't   b doesn't

8   You and Jane _____ French.
    a doesn't speak   b don't speak

9   What _____ after school?
    a does he   b does he do

10 You _____ watch TV in the afternoon.
    a not   b don't

Song

I don't like maths. I'm not good at history
And art and science are a mystery.
But I am good at two special things.
I love pop music and I love to sing.

He doesn't like maths. I don't like history.
I'm good at art and science and geography.
Music is our favourite thing,
When we don't know the words, what do we sing?

La de da be do be
La de da be do be

Vocabulary

Match.

1   playground
2   bookcase
3   classmates
4   cafeteria
5   library
6   uniform

Listening

🎧 **Listen to three children talking about school. Tick (✓) what they like.**

	Eleanor	Paola	Rashid
English lessons			
homework			
teachers			
uniform			
school lunch			
computer lessons			

🎧 **Sounds of English**

A   What's the difference in the oo sounds in these words? Say them, then listen and check your answers.

book   school

B   Read these words and write them in the correct column. Then listen and check your answers.

cool   cook   food   good   look   moon

book   school
_____   _____
_____   _____
_____   _____

33

Reading

Read Anna's letter about her school. When does Anna have dinner?

Anna's School

Dear Vicky,

Thanks for your letter. I'm very happy you're my new penfriend. You haven't got a computer, but it doesn't matter. Letters are also great!

I want to tell you about my school. My school is very different from other schools. I don't go to school every day – I'm already here! I'm a student at Greenwood Boarding School. (1) _____ I've got a room with two other girls. What do I do every day?

I always get up at 7 o'clock. Then I have breakfast with the other students and teachers. We have lessons from 9 till 1 o'clock. Then it's lunch time. (2) _____ After that we usually do our homework.

In the evenings I send emails to my parents. They travel a lot for their work. I also write in my diary. At 6.30 we eat in the dining room. (3) _____ We go to bed at 9.30, but we usually talk until 10.30! This is my school life. What's your school like?

Write soon!

Love,

Anna

Say it like this!

Talking about everyday life

How often do you ...?

I ... every day/week.

I ... once/twice/three times a month/year.

'How often do you use a computer?' 'I use a computer every day.'

Talk to your partner about how often you and your family do these things. Practise the language above.

play computer games   have a test at school
read a book   talk on the phone

Comprehension

Complete the letter with these sentences.

a   In the afternoon we have more lessons until 4 o'clock.

b   After dinner I sometimes watch a DVD with my friends.

c   Pupils sleep here.

Grammar

Adverbs of Frequency

We use adverbs of frequency to show how often we do something.
They often play in the park.

always ⟶ usually ⟶ often ⟶ sometimes ⟶ never
100% of the time ⟵⟶ 0% of the time

Adverbs of frequency go before main verbs.
Dan usually gets up at 7.30 am.

Adverbs of frequency go AFTER the verb *be*.
They are usually at the beach in the afternoon.

A Complete the sentences with adverbs of frequency to make true sentences about you.

1 I _____ get up at 6 am.

2 I _____ do my homework in the morning.

3 I am _____ nice to my parents.

4 I _____ play with my friends after school.

5 Saturdays are _____ fun.

6 My mum is _____ at home in the afternoon.

B Put the adverbs of frequency in the correct place in the sentences.

1 Sam brushes his teeth in the morning. (always)

   _____

2 The boys are hungry at 12 o'clock. (usually)

   _____

3 They don't wear shoes at home. (often)

   _____

4 That shop is open at weekends. (never)

   _____

Writing

Word Order

A Look at the word order in these examples.

I (don't) like sport.
Do you have art lessons once a week?
Is Emma usually at home in the evening?
Mr Brown sometimes wears jeans.
We are always happy at the weekend.
Does Jim often sing at school?

B Put the words in the correct order.

1 science / never / boring / is

   _____

2 ? / you / do / maths / like

   _____

3 often / watch / at weekends / I / DVDs

   _____

4 ? / Mrs Hill / good / a / teacher / is

   _____

5 we / every day / don't / computer games / play

   _____

C Read the paragraph. Find five mistakes with word order and correct them.

My Perfect School
In my perfect school, lessons start at 10 o'clock and they finish at 1 o'clock. We have never maths, English, history or geography. We every day have sport and computer lessons! These are my favourite subjects. We listen often to music in the classroom and we have never tests. The teachers always are nice to us.

Task

D Write a paragraph about your perfect school. Use this plan to help you.

Begin like this: In my perfect school, …

Answer the questions:

What time do lessons start?

_____

What time do they finish?

_____

What lessons do you have?

_____

What subjects do you have every day?

_____

What else is good about this school?

_____

E Read your paragraph and check the word order.

4 Hobbies

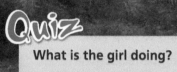

What is the girl doing?

a playing with a horse
b riding a horse
c racing a horse

The Cortuga Mystery

🎧 **Listen and read.**

1
Robbie: Where are we now?
Kate: I don't know.
Jake: That writing is Chinese! We're in China!
Mandy: Look at all those beautiful kites!

2
Robbie: Hello. What's your name?
Ling: Ling. Who are you?
Robbie: I'm Robbie and these are my friends.
Jake: Hi, Ling! What's the matter?
Ling: There's a kite competition today, but I haven't got a kite.
Robbie: It's OK! Let's make a kite!

3
What do we need? There's a shop here.
But we haven't got any Chinese money!
It doesn't matter. It's my uncle's shop!

4
Later...
Kate: Wow! That's fantastic! You're very clever, Robbie.
Robbie: Here you are, Ling.
Ling: It's beautiful. Thanks Robbie!

5
After the competition...
Jake: Who's the winner?
Robbie: Ling is the winner. Congratulations, Ling!
Ling: Thanks. I'm very happy.
Robbie: Me too.
Ling: This is the prize and it's for you!
Robbie: It's a piece of the puzzle!

6
Thanks a lot, Ling!
Bye!!!

Vocabulary

A Match.

1 I'm the winner!   a Me too!
2 Here you are.   b I don't know.
3 What's the matter?   c I haven't got any money.
4 Where are we now?   d Congratulations!
5 I'm happy!   e Thanks.

B Complete the phrases with these words.

collect	go	make	play	watch

1 _____ ice-skating / swimming
2 _____ TV / DVDs
3 _____ the piano / the guitar
4 _____ stamps / coins
5 _____ a kite / a boat

C Which word from exercise B can we also use with the verb fly?

Grammar

Question Words

We use the question word:
a What to ask about things or animals.
   What is that? It's a kite.
   What is this? It's a shark.
b Who to ask about people.
   Who is that boy? That's John.
c Where to ask about places.
   Where is Madrid? It's in Spain.
d Whose to ask about possessions.
   Whose house is it? It's my house.
e When to ask about times and dates.
   When is your birthday? It's on 12th July.

Note: Be careful with the words Who's (Who is) and Whose.

A Match.

1 What's your favourite thing?   a It's near here.
2 Where is the shop?   b That's Betty's friend.
3 Whose calculator is this?   c My computer.
4 When is your music lesson?   d It's Mary's.
5 Who is that tall girl?   e It's every Thursday.

B Look at the answers and write the question words.

1 '_____ colour is your kite?' 'It's red and blue.'
2 '_____ pen is on my desk?' 'Jenny's.'
3 '_____ is the competition?' 'It's on Saturday.'
4 '_____ does Ling live?' 'She lives in China.'
5 '_____ is Miss Jones?' 'She's our aunt.'

Listening

🎧 Listen to Adam talking about his hobbies. Draw lines from the days to the pictures.

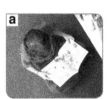

1 Monday

2 Tuesday

3 Wednesday

4 Thursday

5 Friday

Speaking

Talk about your hobby. Ask and answer these questions with your partner.

What's your hobby?
What do you need for your hobby?
Why do you like it?
When do you do it?
Where do you do it?
Who do you do it with?

Writing

Write six sentences about your hobby. Answer the questions in the Speaking task.

Reading

Read about a fantastic amusement park.

Luna Park is a very old and a very popular amusement park in Sydney, Australia. Thousands of visitors and tourists come here every year. At the entrance there is a huge smiling face. It is a very famous face in Australia. You go in through its mouth and you can see its teeth above you!

Luna Park

Rides and Attractions

People of all ages can have fun here. There are many rides like the Wild Mouse rollercoaster. It's very scary! There is also a ferris wheel. On this ride you can get a great view of the amusement park and Sydney harbour. There are also slides, merry-go-rounds and many other attractions like the Crazy Mirrors. Your face and body look very funny in these mirrors. There are also lots of games with fantastic prizes.

Food

There are very nice restaurants and cafés at Luna Park. They've got pizzas, burgers and sandwiches. They also sell ice cream, coffee and drinks.

Cost

You can get in for free, but you pay for the rides. A single ride ticket is $10 but for hours of fun buy a *Go Wild* pass. It costs only $48. You can use it all day and enjoy all rides.

Guess what!

The Kingda rollercoaster in the USA is 139 metres high and travels at 205 kilometres an hour!

Comprehension

Answer the questions.

1 What is Luna Park?
   _____

2 Where is the famous face?
   _____

3 Who can have a great time at Luna Park?
   _____

4 What food is there at Luna Park?
   _____

5 What do you pay for at Luna Park?
   _____

Vocabulary

Find the words in the text and write the missing letters.

1 This is a door or a place you go in.   e _ _ _ _ _ _ _

2 These are people on holiday.   t _ _ _ _ _ _ _ _

3 This is something very big.   h _ _ _ _

4 You go on these at amusement parks.   r _ _ _ _

5 You can look at your face in this.   m _ _ _ _ _

Grammar

Can

We use can to:
a talk about ability.
Brian can swim.
b ask for and give permission.
Can I watch TV?
You can go out and play.

We use a bare infinitive (verb without *to*, eg *do*, *go*, *read*) after can.

Affirmative

I/You/He/She/It/We/They can swim.

Negative

I/You/He/She/It/We/They can't (cannot) swim.

Question

Can I/you/he/she/it/we/they swim?

Short Answers

Yes, I/you/he/she/it/we/they can.
No, I/you/he/she/it/we/they can't.

A Complete the sentences with can or can't.

1 My mum _____ speak Chinese.

2 I _____ write my name in English.

3 Dogs _____ read.

4 Teddy bears _____ play the piano.

5 A baby _____ read a comic.

B Ask for permission and give short answers for these things.

1 I / play computer games

_____ ?

_____ (✓)

2 we / go to bed at 2 am

_____ ?

_____ (✗)

3 they / use mobile phones at school

_____ ?

_____ (✗)

4 she / go to the beach

_____ ?

_____ (✓)

5 he / have a cat

_____ ?

_____ (✗)

C Ask your teacher for permission to do things at school.

Vocabulary

Match the places with the sentences.

> amusement park   cinema   restaurant
> sports centre   theatre   Internet café

1 You can have dinner here.   _____

2 You can send emails here.   _____

3 You can see a film here.   _____

4 You can play basketball here.   _____

5 You can go on rides here.   _____

6 You can see a play here.   _____

Listening

🎧 **Listen to Vicky and Rachel and circle the correct words.**

1 Rachel doesn't like amusement parks / films.

2 Vicky wants to see a film at the cinema / home.

3 Vicky thinks the park is boring / cold.

4 Vicky's text message is from Jane / Emma.

5 Jane and Emma are at school / the Internet café.

🎧 **Sounds of English**

A Read the words aloud. Which two words don't have a w sound at the beginning? Listen and check your answers.

when
who
where
what
whose

B Write S (same) or D (different) for the letters in red. Then listen and check your answers.

1 who, hobby ☐

2 when, house ☐

3 what, wood ☐

4 whose, walk ☐

5 where, we ☐

Reading

Read the dialogue. Who meets his friends on Saturdays?

What do YOU do on Saturdays?

Dimitris: Hi, I'm Dimitris. Where are you from?

Eric: Hi! My name's Eric. I'm from London, but I'm in Greece for a week.

Dimitris: Nice to meet you.

Eric: Nice to meet you, too. What do you usually do here on Saturdays?

Dimitris: Well, in the summer I go swimming and then I eat a big meal with my family. And you?

Eric: Well, my dad's got a bike shop and on Saturday mornings I help in the shop.

Dimitris: Wow! That's fantastic! What do you do on Saturday evenings?

Eric: I sometimes go to the sports centre with my friends and we go bowling. We also have competitions. I'm very good at bowling. Do you go bowling?

Dimitris: No, I don't. I often go to the cinema with my parents on Saturday. In Greece you can see films at cinemas outside in the summer!

Eric: Really? We can't do that in England. Do you play computer games?

Dimitris: Yes, I do. I've got a computer at home.

Eric: Well, I haven't got a computer but I often go to an Internet café at the weekend. It's great! You can play computer games and send emails there.

Dimitris: Eric, can I have you email address?

Eric: Yes, of course. Here you are.

Dimitris: We can be e-pals.

Eric: That's a good idea!

Comprehension

Write D (Dimitris) or E (Eric). On Saturdays, who ...

1 works? ☐
2 eats a lot? ☐
3 goes out with friends? ☐
4 sees a film? ☐
5 goes out with family? ☐

Say it like this!

Talking about hobbies

Do you like + verb + -ing?
Do you like bowling?

Are you good at + verb + -ing?
Are you good at bowling?

Talk to your partner about different hobbies. Practise the language above.

Listening

🎧 **Listen to the telephone message and complete the cinema information.**

Star Cinema 1

Film: 'My Crazy (1) _____'

(2) exciting ☐   funny ☐

Times: (3) _____ pm and 9 pm

Star Cinema 2

Film: 'The (4) _____'

(5) exciting ☐   funny ☐

(6) For: adults ☐   children ☐

Speaking

Look at the pictures and say what Mick:
a   is or isn't good at.
b   can or can't do.

Writing

Verb Forms

A   Look at the structures in these examples.

1   Mum and I go shopping on Saturdays.

2   Do you like playing in the park?

3   Jan can speak English and French.

4   His brother is good at making kites.

B   Circle the correct words.

1   I can fly / flying a kite.

2   Ben doesn't like read / reading books.

3   Are you good at riding / ride a bike?

4   We go ice-skate / ice-skating on Friday.

C   Complete Liam's letter to his new penfriend with these verbs in the correct form.

> collect   go   play   swim   swim

Dear Bianca,

My name is Liam Brown and I'm 11 years old. I live in London with my parents and my brother Fred. He's six years old. In my free time I like (1) _____ stamps and (2) _____ computer games. I also (3) _____ swimming on Saturdays. I am good at (4) _____ and I can (5) _____ very fast.

Write soon and tell me about you!

Liam

Task

D   Choose one of these penfriends and write a letter to him or her. Use this plan to help you.

Connie, 9, Holland

Keith, 12, Australia

Begin like this:
Dear _____,

Answer these questions:
What's your name?

_____

How old are you?

_____

Where do you live?

_____

Who do you live with?

_____

What do you like to do in your free time?

_____

What can you also do?

_____

Finish like this:
Write soon!
_____ (your name)

E   Read your letter and check the verb forms.

Review 2

Vocabulary

A Find the stickers.

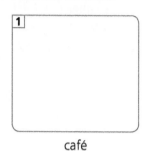

1 café

2 entrance

3 ferris wheel

4 harbour

5 merry-go-round

6 mirror

7 rollercoaster

8 slide

B Circle the odd one out.

1 library	theatre	cinema
2 uniform	sum	jeans
3 ice-skating	swimming	shopping
4 sandwich	coffee	pizza
5 science	history	bowling
6 kite	coins	money
7 visitor	tourist	classmate
8 calculator	maths	club

C Match.

1	watch	a	an email
2	sing	b	your teeth
3	send	c	stamps
4	make	d	songs
5	do	e	a kite
6	brush	f	your homework
7	collect	g	a uniform
8	wear	h	TV

Grammar

A Choose the correct answers.

1 My brothers _____ to boarding school.
   a goes
   b go

2 _____ like amusement parks?
   a You
   b Do you

3 We _____ have homework every day.
   a don't
   b not

4 'Does Ryan have breakfast every morning?'
   'Yes, he _____.'
   a has
   b does

5 I usually _____ up at 10 o' clock on Saturdays.
   a gets
   b get

6 My cat can't _____ many tricks.
   a do
   b doing

7 I don't like _____ my homework.
   a doing
   b do

8 His brother is very good at _____ computer games.
   a plays
   b playing

B Put the words in the correct order.

1 school / never / on Saturday / go / we / to

_____

2 my / I / write / diary / in / usually / every day

_____

3 isn't / geography / boring / always

_____

4 karate clubs / have / sometimes / Japanese schools

_____

5 scary / often / rollercoasters / are

_____

6 ? / eat / you / lunch / do / always / at school

_____

C The words in bold are wrong. Write the correct words.

1 '**Who** is that calculator?'
'It's Mike's.' _____

2 '**What** is my money?'
'It's on the table.' _____

3 '**Where** does the film start?'
'At 9 o'clock.' _____

4 '**When** is the prize?'
'It's 200 euros.' _____

5 '**Whose** is Yuko?'
'She's my Japanese penfriend.' _____

6 '**Who's** boat is this?
'It's our boat.' _____

D Write short answers.

1 Can you play the piano?

_____

2 Can your mum use a computer?

_____

3 Can your friends go to Internet cafés?

_____

4 Can your dad speak English?

_____

5 Can you and your classmates have lunch at school?

_____

6 Can you watch TV late at night?

_____

Song

What do you do on Saturday?
Do you go shopping? Do you play?
It's fantastic! We don't have school
And Luna Park is really cool.
It's fun! It's exciting! It's scary too!
On the Ferris Wheel, look at the view.

Go up, go fast on the rollercoaster.
Go round on the merry-go-round.
Fly like a kite in the sky.
Ride up and then slide down.
We can have fun on Saturdays.
But Luna Park is open every day.

MONKEY'S P

Quiz

Why are there parties
for monkeys in Thailand?
Because people say that
monkeys

a   are important.

b   are hungry.

c   like parties.

Vocabulary

Complete the sentences with these words.

> catch   festival   paint   stall   throw

1 Don't _____ the ball near the window.
2 People can dance and sing at a _____ .
3 _____ that dog! It's got my shoe.
4 Have you got any red _____?
5 Let's buy food from that _____ .

Grammar

Imperative

We use the imperative to give instructions to someone else. We form the imperative with a bare infinitive. We often use please with imperatives. We use Don't to make a negative imperative.

Affirmative	Negative
Please be careful!	Don't go to the party!

What does the teacher say? Circle the correct words.

1 Not play / Don't play loud music!
2 Don't move / Move not the desks!
3 Please clean / to clean the classroom after the party!
4 Don't is / be late for school again, Tara!

Object Pronouns

We use object pronouns to replace the object of a sentence.
I've got two cats. I love them!

Subject Pronouns	Object Pronouns
I	me
he/she/it	him/her/it
we/you/they	us/you/them

Complete the dialogue with the correct object pronouns.

Claire: Happy Birthday, Sally!
Sally: Thanks! What's this?
Claire: It's a present from (1) _____ .
Sally: A T-shirt! Great! Thanks!
Claire: Do you like the colours?
Sally: Yes, I love (2) _____ !
Claire: Happy Birthday from Paul, too.
Sally: Thanks! Let's send (3) _____ a photo of the two of (4) _____ .
Claire: OK! Smile!

Let's

We use Let's with a bare infinitive to make suggestions.
Let's eat.
It's hot. Let's go to the beach!

Make suggestions using Let's and these verbs.

> dance   go   have   play   swim

1 I've got a new board game. _____ .
2 This music's very good. _____ .
3 This party's boring. _____ home.
4 The sea isn't cold today. _____ .
5 It's a holiday. _____ fun.

Vocabulary

Write the correct words under the pictures.

> balloons   cake   candles   card   invitation   party hat

_____   _____   _____

_____   _____   _____

Listening

🎧 **Listen to Jan and Toby talking about their plans for a party. Tick (✓) the correct boxes.**

Things for my party:

	Jan	Toby
1 make invitations	☐	☐
2 CDs	☐	☐
3 a camera	☐	☐
4 buy balloons	☐	☐
5 make a cake	☐	☐

Speaking

Talk to your partner and make suggestions about things to do on these days. Use Let's and these phrases to help you.

> buy a present   dance   go to the beach
> have a party   make a cake   play games

1 New Year
2 your friend's birthday
3 school holidays
4 a festival

Writing

Write five sentences about preparations for a party.

Carnival Crazy!

Reading

Read about a fantastic carnival. What clothes do people wear in the carnival?

The Patras Carnival in Greece is very famous. About 40,000 people take part in the carnival and they have a lot of fun! There are parades for children and adults. People wear costumes, funny hats and masks and they dance in the streets!

There are lots of other events too. At carnival workshops, children make models out of paper and paint them. There are also treasure hunts! The treasure is in a secret place in the city of Patras and groups of people look for it. There are some clues in different places to help them! The winners get great prizes.

On the last night of the carnival, people burn the Carnival King. It's OK, he isn't a real person! There are lots of fireworks, music and dancing. Soon preparations start for next year's carnival!

"The Great Carnival Parade of Children in Patras, Greece, 2008"
Photographer: Antonis Tsiliras

Guess what!
Canada has a winter carnival. The 'king' of the carnival is a giant snowman.

Comprehension

Circle the correct words.

1 There are usually 40,000 parades / **people** at the Patras Carnival.
2 You can dance / **make** things at carnival workshops.
3 People look for costumes / **treasure** at the Patras Carnival.
4 People have **clues** / prizes to find the treasure.
5 The Carnival King **is** / **isn't** a real person.

Vocabulary

Circle the odd one out.

1	carnival	festival	clue
2	fireworks	parades	preparations
3	children	treasure	adult
4	city	street	model
5	costume	place	mask

Grammar

Countable Nouns

Countable nouns are nouns that we can count. We can use them in the singular and the plural.
They need a costume.
Let's buy three hats.

Uncountable Nouns

Uncountable nouns are nouns that we cannot count and that haven't got plurals. We use a singular verb after these nouns. We don't use a/an with uncountable nouns.
There is music at the carnival.

Complete the sentences with a, an or – (if no word is needed).

1 Have you got _____ mask for the carnival?
2 We need _____ money for the balloons.
3 This is _____ invitation to my party.
4 I want _____ fireworks at my party!
5 The carnival king has got _____ hair.
6 There is _____ parade for children on Saturday.

Vocabulary

Match.

1 mask ☐
2 pirate ☐
3 witch ☐
4 clown ☐
5 cowboy ☐
6 magician ☐
7 king ☐
8 queen ☐

Listening

🎧 **Listen and match the costumes with the children. There is one costume that you do not need to use.**

Monster   King   Clown

Witch   Queen

1 Suzy _____
2 Nicky _____
3 Mel _____
4 Sam _____

🎧 **Sounds of English**

A Listen and circle the words you hear.

1 shoe / Sue
2 she / sea
3 sort / short
4 show / so

B Listen and then try this tongue twister!

Sid's shop sells silver shoes!

Reading

Read the article. Whose pet doesn't like something?

Bonfire Night
(Sophie, 9, England)

Bonfire Night is my favourite night of the year. It's on November 5th and it's always very cold! My dad makes a big fire outside and we eat hot food next to the fire. Then we have some fireworks. Our cat stays in the house because she's scared of them!

Special Days Around the World

April Fool's Day
(Pascal, 10, France)

On 1st April I play jokes on my friends and family. I sometimes change the time on my sister's watch and she's late for school! Then I call her an 'April Fish' – that means 'April Fool' in France. At school we play jokes on the teacher or the teacher plays jokes on us. The teachers sometimes give us a test but we know it's April Fool's Day and we just laugh.

Australia Day
(Ed, 11, Australia)

Australia Day is great. It's on 26th January every year. We celebrate our country and everything that is good about it. It's a holiday, so we don't go to school. There are fireworks and parades and people have parties. We don't have a party in the house. We have a barbecue on the beach with our cousins. It's great!

Say it like this!

Making suggestions

Why don't you + bare infinitive ...?
'Why don't you have a party for your national day?'

Talk to your partner about a party. Practise making suggestions.

Comprehension

Complete the table.

Bonfire Night	April Fool's Day	Australia Day
make a (1) _____	play (3) _____	celebrate (5) _____
watch (2) _____	call people (4) _____	have a (6) _____

Grammar

Some / any

We use some in affirmative sentences with plural countable and uncountable nouns.
I've got some presents!
There's some food on the table.

We use any in negative sentences and questions with plural countable and uncountable nouns.
There aren't any masks in this shop.
Have you got any paper?

A Complete the sentences with some or any.

1 Is there _____ yellow paint?

2 Mum has got _____ silver shoes.

3 We usually have _____ fireworks at New Year.

4 Grandad doesn't go to _____ carnivals.

5 Have the children got _____ money?

B Complete the dialogue with some or any.

John: Kay, I need (1) _____ things. Have you got (2) _____ lemonade?

Kay: No, but I've got (3) _____ orange juice.

John: OK. Orange juice is fine. I also need (4) _____ balloons and paper.

Kay: There's lots of paper in the house but there aren't (5) _____ balloons. Go and buy them.

John: I can't because I haven't got (6) _____ money. One last question. Have you got (7) _____ stamps?

Kay: Yes, but why do you need all these things?

John: Well, I want to have a party and I want to invite (8) _____ friends.

Kay: Really? Well, it's my party too now. Let's start preparations.

Writing

Reference Words

A Read about reference words.

We use reference words instead of repeating nouns. They make writing sound better! Subject and object pronouns are reference words.

B Replace the words in blue with subject or object pronouns.

1 I've got a clown costume. Do you like my clown costume?

2 Where are the candles? Are the candles here?

3 It's Tessa's birthday. Let's make a cake for Tessa!

4 The prize is for Jodie and me! Jodie and I are the winners!

5 Dad doesn't know it's April Fool's Day. Let's play a joke on Dad!

C Replace the phrases in red with reference words.

My Birthday

On my birthday I always have a party. I invite all my friends to my party and my friends and I have a great time! My mum usually makes a birthday cake. The birthday cake is always chocolate and the birthday cake is fantastic! My friends come to my house in the evening and my friends bring me presents. Then my friends and I eat, play CDs and dance!

Task

D Write a paragraph about what you do at a family party. Use the questions below to help you.

Answer the questions:

Do you have a party every year?

_____

Who do you usually invite? (friends, cousins, uncles, aunts, etc)

_____

Do you have a cake?

_____

Who makes it? What kind of cake is it?

_____

Do you eat and drink other things?

_____

What do your friends bring?

_____

What do you do at the party?

_____

E Remember to use reference words instead of repeating some nouns.

6 Food!

Quiz

What is the name of a baby deer?

a doe

b fawn

c stag

6 Lesson 1

🎧 **Listen and read.**

1
Jake: Look! It's 2050!
Kate: We're in the future! Amazing!
Mandy: Yes, but I'm hungry.
Robbie: Me too! Look, there's a fast food restaurant over there!
Mandy: Come on! I like fast food.

2
Mandy: Wow! A robot.
Jake: There aren't many things on the menu.
Robot: Can I help you?
Robbie: Yes, we'd like two burgers, some chips and two cheese and tomato sandwiches, please.
Mandy: Some ketchup and a glass of orange juice, too.

3
Robot: Here you are.
Robbie: Where's the food? They're just pills!
Robot: Food? People don't eat food.
Robbie: But real food is delicious!
Robot: Maybe. But meals are easy with pills. You don't need much time for preparation.
Robbie: Yes, but these pills aren't tasty. Yuk!

4
Jake: Look at that menu on the table!
Kate: There's a piece of the puzzle on it.
Robot: I see rubbish! Throw it in this bag, please.
Robbie: But I want it. Can I have it?
Robot: OK. You're a strange boy.

5
Robbie: Thanks a lot. Look, this is some special food from 2009.
Robot: What is it?
Robbie: It's called chewing gum. Here you are.
Robot: System error ... repeat ... system error!
Mandy: Look! The robot can't move its hands.
Robbie: Oh, no! I'm sorry! I can help you. Look, it's OK now.

6
Have you got the piece?
Yes. Time to go!
OK.

56

Vocabulary

Circle the correct words.

1 I'm delicious / hungry. What's for lunch?
2 Have you got any orange / chewing juice?
3 Pills / Burgers are my favourite food!
4 Can I have a glass of chips / water, please?
5 Let's eat a sandwich / menu at the café.

Grammar

Much, Many

We use much and many to describe quantities.

We use much in negative sentences and questions with uncountable nouns.
I don't want much juice.
Have you got much food?

We use many in affirmative and negative sentences and questions with plural countable nouns.
The restaurant has got many menus.
I haven't got many chips.
Are there many people at the cafè?

Note: We don't usually use many in affirmative sentences. We can use lots of or a lot of instead of many or much.
There are lots of sandwiches on the table.
My brother eats lots of food.

We use how much and how many to ask about quantities.
How much water is there?
How many burgers do you want?

Note: We can use How much ...? to ask about prices.
How much is the orange juice? It's one euro.

Complete the sentences with many or much.

1 There isn't _____ rubbish in the house.
2 How _____ sandwiches has Henry got?
3 Do you eat _____ cakes?
4 I haven't got _____ chewing gum.
5 They haven't got _____ tomatoes.

Vocabulary

Write the correct words.

| bill | dessert | drink | fast food | menu | plate | snack | waiter |

1 This man works in a restaurant.   _____
2 This tells you about the food in a restaurant.   _____
3 You can eat this after your meal.   _____
4 Burgers and chips are this.   _____
5 You eat your meal on this.   _____
6 The waiter gives you this at the end of a meal. _____
7 Orange juice is this.   _____
8 This isn't a big meal.   _____

Listening

🎧 **Listen and tick (✓) the correct pictures.**

1 What is delicious?

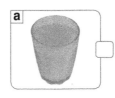 

2 What does the boy want?

3 What does the waiter bring?

 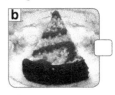

4 What does the woman want?

 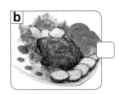

5 What does the girl want?

 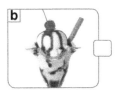

Speaking

Talk to your partner about your favourite restaurant or café. Use these words to help you.

amazing   delicious   drinks   famous   food
great   music   nice   people   tasty   waiters

Writing

Write six sentences about your favourite restaurant or café. Answer these questions.

What's its name?
Who goes there?
What food and drinks has it got?
What do you usually eat and drink there?
How often do you go there?
Why do you like it?

Reading

Read about food. Which letter means yes?

What can food tell us?

Bananas

Take a banana and ask a question. Only ask questions with a yes or a no answer. Then cut the banana in two with a knife. Is there a 'Y' in the middle of the banana? The answer to your question is yes! You can't see a 'Y'? Then the answer is no!

Tea

Have a nice cup of tea with your breakfast. Drink the tea and then look at the tea leaves in the cup. What do they look like? A moon means good times. Or maybe they look like animals. A duck means money and a fish means health and happiness!

Cheese

Make a wish. Then cut a slice of Swiss cheese. This is the cheese with holes. How many holes are there in the cheese? Are there just a few holes? You've only got a few weeks before your wish comes true! A lot of holes mean a long wait!

Apples

Hold the stalk (see arrow in picture) of an apple, turn the apple and say the alphabet. The letter you say when the apple falls is the first letter of your future friend's name.

Guess what!

There is a mustard museum in the USA. It has got 4,900 different kinds of mustard!

Comprehension

Write T (true) or F (false).

1 Bananas always have a 'Y' in the middle. ☐

2 Swiss cheese has got holes in it. ☐

3 You drink the tea and the leaves. ☐

4 You can sometimes find a fish in your tea. ☐

5 You can find the first letter of a name with an apple. ☐

Vocabulary

Complete the word groups.

banana   cup   juice   knife   lunch

1 fork, spoon, _____

2 glass, plate, _____

3 tea, coffee, _____

4 cheese, apple, _____

5 breakfast, dinner, _____

Grammar

A lot of, Lots of, A few, A little

We use a lot of or lots of with countable and uncountable nouns in affirmative and negative sentences and questions.
We haven't got a lot of bananas!
Have you got a lot of money?

We use a few with countable nouns in affirmative sentences and questions.
There are a few restaurants here.
Do you want a few chips?

We use a little with uncountable nouns in affirmative sentences and questions.
There is a little water.
Can I have a little cheese, please?

Look at the picture and complete the sentences with a lot of, a few or a little.

1 There are _____ sandwiches.

2 There is _____ orange juice.

3 There are _____ bananas.

4 There is _____ water.

5 There are _____ cakes.

Vocabulary

Match.

1 chicken ☐
2 butter ☐
3 chocolate ☐
4 bread ☐
5 rice ☐
6 milk ☐
7 spaghetti ☐
8 meat ☐

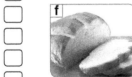

Listening

🎧 **What do they need to buy for the picnic? Listen and tick (✓) or cross (✗) the things on the shopping list.**

☐ eggs
☐ bread
☐ apples
☐ bananas
☐ chocolate

🎧 Sounds of English

A Read these pairs of words aloud.

1 which ☐   wish ☐
2 cheese ☐   she's ☐
3 chew ☐   shoe ☐
4 chip ☐   ship ☐
5 watch ☐   wash ☐

B Now listen and tick the words you hear.

Song

I am hungry. I want chicken and chips,
Or fish and chips or meat and chips.
Sometimes I like eggs and chips.
Chips are always good.

For a snack I like tomato sandwiches,
Swiss cheese sandwiches, chicken sandwiches,
Cheese and egg and ketchup sandwiches.
Snacks are my favourite food.

For breakfast I like chicken and chocolate
Chewing gum and chocolate, chips and chocolate.
Then, for lunch, spaghetti and chocolate.
Chocolate's delicious food.

Reading

Read the fact sheet. Which food is not nice for some people?

Food around the World

Scotland

People in Scotland eat a lot of hot food because it's cold. They also like food from other countries. There are a lot of Indian and Chinese restaurants. Fish and chips is their favourite food. It's fast food, but it's delicious! People in Scotland are also crazy about biscuits.

France

France has got a lot of good food. It is famous for croissants and frogs' legs. Many people from other countries don't like frogs' legs. A popular snack in France is pisaladiere. That's a type of pizza with onions and olives instead of cheese and tomato. For dessert the French love crepes (pancakes) with chocolate and banana.

Spain

In Spain people eat a lot of fish. Paella is a famous Spanish dish. It's very healthy food and it has got chicken, fish and rice. There are also a lot of tapas restaurants in Spain. In these restaurants the waiter brings lots of different snacks on small plates. Tapas are great!

USA

Americans like Italian food very much. Pizza is one of their favourite foods. Spaghetti (long pasta) with cheese and tomato sauce is also very popular in the USA because it's delicious and easy to cook. We all know that people in the USA eat lots of burgers. Other popular foods are French fries (chips) and fried chicken.

Comprehension

Complete the sentences with words from the fact sheet.

1 In Scotland people like Indian and _____ food.

2 Fish and chips is _____ food.

3 A popular French snack is a pizza with olives onions and _____ .

4 Paella has got chicken, fish and _____ in it.

5 In the USA French fries and _____ chicken are also popular foods.

Say it like this!

Talking about food

What's your favourite food?
I love … .
'What's your favourite food?' 'I love spaghetti.'

What about …?
Mmm, it's delicious.
'What about pizza?' 'Mmm, it's delicious.'

How often do you eat …?
Every Saturday/week/day.
Twice/Three times a week.
'How often do you eat meat?' 'Three times a week.'

Talk to your partner about food. Practise the language above.

Listening

🎧 Listen and number the pictures in the correct order.

a

d

b

e

c

f

Speaking

Read the dialogue with your partner. Then change the red words to make your own dialogue. Practise it with your partner.

Jack: What's your favourite food?
Polly: (1) **Chips**.
Jack: How often do you eat (2) **them**?
Polly: (3) **Once a month**.
Jack: Who cooks (4) **them**?
Polly: (5) **My mum**.
Jack: (6) **Are they healthy**?
Polly: (7) **No, they're not**!

Writing

Time words: order of events

A Read about time words.

We use time words to describe the order of actions.

B Number these words in the correct order.

then / after that ☐

finally ☐

first ☐

C Complete the recipe with these words.

After   Finally   First   Then

Banana Sandwich

You need: two slices of bread, one banana, a little butter

(1) _____ cut the banana into slices.
(2) _____ put some butter on the slices of bread. (3) _____ that put the slices of banana between the two slices of bread. (4) _____ eat the sandwich!

Task ✏

D Write a recipe for your favourite snack. Use the questions below to help you.

What's the name of the snack?

_____

What do you need?

_____

Which verbs do you need for your recipe?

cook cut make put slice use wash

_____

E Read your recipe and check the time words.

Vocabulary

A Complete the table.

> balloons bill candles cowboy invitation
> menu pirate waiter witch

Costumes	Birthday party	Restaurant
_____	_____	_____
_____	_____	_____
_____	_____	_____

B Choose the correct answers.

1 Let's _____ a joke on dad!
   a play
   b make

2 'Do you like Chinese food?' 'Yes, it's _____!'
   a real
   b delicious

3 Look at the time! We're _____ for school!
   a healthy
   b late

4 I'm not very hungry. I just want a _____ .
   a meal
   b snack

5 Burgers and chips are _____ food.
   a quiet
   b fast

6 Follow the _____ and find the treasure!
   a clues
   b prizes

7 Look at the _____ in the sky. They're great.
   a preparations
   b fireworks

8 There are a lot of people in the _____ .
   a parade
   b mask

C Find the stickers.

1	2
biscuits	bread

3	4
butter	chewing gum

5	6
chicken	meat

7	8
knife	plate

Grammar

A Find the mistake in each sentence. Write the correct sentences.

1 Let's going to the party!

   _____

2 Not drink that orange juice!

   _____

3 Let's to have a picnic on Saturday!

   _____

4 Doesn't watch the fireworks!

   _____

5 Enjoys her birthday!

   _____

6 Don't laughing in the library!

   _____

B Write a, an or some.

1 _____ sandwich

2 _____ drink

3 _____ music

4 _____ apple

5 _____ cheese

6 _____ restaurant

7 _____ monster

8 _____ money

C Circle the correct words.

1 I haven't got any / a little chewing gum!

2 How much / many eggs do you want for breakfast?

3 I don't eat much / a lot chocolate.

4 Can I have a few / little chips with my burger?

5 There are some / any cups in the kitchen.

6 There is only a few / a little rubbish my room.

7 They always buy a lot of / lots orange juice.

8 How many / much cakes do you need for the party?

D The words in bold are wrong. Write the correct words.

1 My sister loves fireworks, but I don't like **it**. _____

2 That man's a clown. Look at **her**! _____

3 That invitation is from **you**. It's for my party on Saturday. _____

4 This present is great! I love **him**! _____

5 We want to play! Throw the ball to **them**! _____

6 Let's go to that stall. There are paints on **me**. _____

7 Jane's ten today! Let's buy **us** a cake. _____

8 I like you and Mike so I want to give **me** some CDs. _____

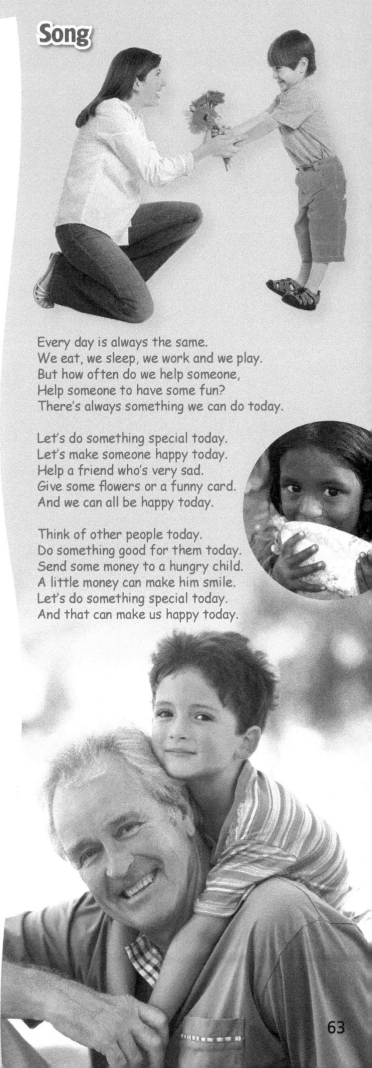

Song

Every day is always the same.
We eat, we sleep, we work and we play.
But how often do we help someone,
Help someone to have some fun?
There's always something we can do today.

Let's do something special today.
Let's make someone happy today.
Help a friend who's very sad.
Give some flowers or a funny card.
And we can all be happy today.

Think of other people today.
Do something good for them today.
Send some money to a hungry child.
A little money can make him smile.
Let's do something special today.
And that can make us happy today.

7 Sport

Quiz

What is the woman climbing?

a   a frozen waterfall

b   a frozen wall

c   a frozen river

🎧 **Listen and read.**

The Cortuga Mystery

Egg and Spoon Race ENTER HERE

1
Jake:	Where are we now?
Kate:	What a beautiful park!
Mandy:	Look! Those people are having a picnic.
Robbie:	And they're playing games. Let's go and play too!

2
Robbie:	Let's enter the egg and spoon race.
Jake:	Yes, it's great fun! Come on, girls!
Kate:	Not me. What about you, Mandy?
Mandy:	No, thanks. We can watch you.
Jake:	Look! There's a piece of the puzzle under the trophy.

START

3
Referee:	OK. Put your eggs on your spoons.
Jake:	Hey, you! Stop that! Why are you pushing me?
Robbie:	Leave him alone!
Simon:	Sorry! It's just that I want to win the race. I never win.
Referee:	Get ready, set, go!

4
Mandy:	Look, Kate! Jake is in front.
Kate:	And Robbie is running just behind him.
Mandy:	Go, Jake, go!
Kate:	Oh, no! A dog's chasing Robbie. The egg is falling off his spoon.
Mandy:	Yuk! The egg is on his shoes now.
Kate:	Yes, but look at Jake! He's a fast runner.
Mandy:	Jake is crossing the finishing line with that boy!

5
Referee:	Congratulations! You are the winner! Here's your prize.
Robbie:	But this boy is also the winner.
Simon:	Yes, I am!
Jake:	OK! You can have the trophy. I just want that!

We're going again!

6

Don't drop the piece of the puzzle, Jake!

Vocabulary

Complete the sentences with these words.

> cross   drop   enter   leave   push

1 Stand behind me and don't _____ me!
2 _____ me alone!
3 My friends _____ this competition every year.
4 I want to _____ the finishing line first!
5 Do you sometimes _____ your spoon?

Grammar

Present Continuous

We use the Present Continuous for actions that are happening now.
They are watching TV now.

Affirmative

I'm (I am) playing.
You're (You are) playing.
He's (He is) playing.
She's (She is) playing.
It's (It is) playing.
We're (We are) playing.
You're (You are) playing.
They're (They are) playing.

Spelling rules

run	running
come	coming
lie	lying

Time expressions

now
at the moment

A Write the verbs with -ing.

1 chase _____
2 fly _____
3 keep _____
4 sit _____
5 wear _____
6 give _____
7 stay _____
8 stop _____

B Complete the sentences with the Present Continuous of the verbs in brackets.

1 Anita _____ (lie) on the sofa.
2 Simon and Jake _____ (run) in the park.
3 A dog _____ (chase) a ball.
4 He _____ (swim) in the sea at the moment.
5 I _____ (play) volleyball with my friends.
6 You _____ (go) to the park.

Vocabulary

Match.

Horse

Bike

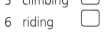
Boat

Boots

Trainers

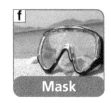
Mask

1 cycling ☐
2 running ☐
3 sailing ☐
4 diving ☐
5 climbing ☐
6 riding ☐

Listening

🎧 **Listen and write the numbers next to the sports.**

climbing ☐   cycling ☐   running ☐
sailing ☐   riding ☐

Speaking

Talk about the people in the picture with your partner.

Writing

Write 5 sentences about the picture in the Speaking task.

Thai Boxing

Reading

Read the article. Does Manat win the fight?

In Thailand, everyone loves Thai boxing. (1) _____ Thai boxing is different from boxing in other countries. You can use your hands and arms, but you can also kick. You must be strong too.

Twelve-year-old Manat is a student at a Thai Boxing training camp. (2) _____ At the camp, he practises for seven hours a day, seven days a week! He trains hard because he wants to be a champion. Champions get money as a prize. (3) _____

Now Manat is getting ready for his second fight. He is calm and he is only thinking about the fight because he wants to win! (4) _____ Yes!

(5) _____ Manat is very good, but he doesn't win the match this time. He is sad, but he isn't giving up. He can still be a champion!

Guess what!
Many Japanese Sumo wrestlers eat fast food because it makes them fat!

Comprehension

Complete the article with these sentences.

a   Is he feeling excited?

b   It's on TV every day.

c   It's the night of the fight.

d   Then he can send this money to his family.

e   It's a training camp for men, women and boys.

Vocabulary

Circle the correct words.

1   Can I use / make your bike, please?

2   I train / kick every night after school.

3   We are helping / getting ready for the match.

4   Don't think / give up! You're winning!

5   Gavin is feeling / practising scared about the fight.

Grammar

Present Continuous

Negative

I'm not (am not) playing.
You aren't (are not) playing.
He/She/It isn't (is not) playing.
We/You/They aren't (are not) playing.
He isn't playing basketball now.

Question

Am I playing?
Are you playing?
Is he/she/it playing?
Are we/you/they playing?
Are you playing in the school team?

Short answers

Yes, I am.
Yes, you/we/they are.
Yes, he/she/it is.
Is he kicking the ball?

No, I'm not.
No, you/we/they aren't.
No, he/she/it isn't.
Yes, he is.

Match.

1 Is Samantha watching a boxing match?
2 Are your mum and dad playing tennis?
3 Is Paul wearing a helmet?
4 Is the horse feeling scared?
5 Am I winning?

a No, it isn't.
b Yes, they are.
c No, she isn't.
d No, you aren't.
e Yes, he is.

Vocabulary

Match.

1 gymnast ☐
2 boxer ☐
3 footballer ☐
4 tennis player ☐
5 cyclist ☐
6 swimmer ☐

Listening

🎧 Listen to two children playing the game 'Who am I?' and write Y (yes) or N (no).

The mystery person:

1 is a woman. ☐
2 is a tennis player. ☐
3 is English. ☐
4 is living in England. ☐
5 has got a famous wife. ☐

🎧 Sounds of English

A Listen and underline the word you hear.

1	leave	live
2	feet	fit
3	Tim	team
4	eat	it
5	ship	sheep
6	feel	fill

B Practise saying the pairs of words in A.

Song

It's great! We're training on the beach.
It looks like a big party on the beach.
No. No. It isn't raining on the beach.
The sun is shining up in the sky.

Lots of people are sailing on the sea.
Some children are climbing up a tree.
Those girls are diving in the sea.
The boys are running on the sand.

The football team is practising again.
They're having a big match next weekend.
The swimming team is racing today.
They're getting ready for a competition.

Reading

Read the interview with Robin and Laura. How many times do they practise a day?

Ice Dancers

Robin and Laura are Britain's junior ice dancing champions. What are they training for at the moment?

Reporter:	How old are you?
Laura:	I'm fourteen and Robin's thirteen.
Reporter:	Tell me about your day.
Laura:	We get up at six o'clock every morning and we practise for an hour before school.
Robin:	Then after school we practise again for two hours!
Reporter:	It's hard work, then!
Laura:	Yes, but we love it. We want to be Olympic champions!
Reporter:	Are you training at the moment?
Robin:	Yes, we are. We're training for a big competition in London next week.
Laura:	Our coach is teaching us new things for the competition. They're very difficult.
Reporter:	Are you excited about the competition?
Robin:	Yes! Young ice skaters from many countries are coming. It's very exciting.
Reporter:	What music are you skating to?
Laura:	It's from the film The Lion King.
Reporter:	Well, good luck!
Robin and Laura:	Thanks!

Comprehension

Answer the questions.

1 What time do Robin and Laura get up?

_____

2 How many hours a day do they practise?

_____

3 What do Robin and Laura want to be?

_____

4 What is happening next week?

_____

5 What is from *The Lion King*?

_____

Say it like this!

Talking about sport

Who's your favourite ... player?
I'm a ... fan!
'Who's your favourite football player?' 'I'm a Ronaldo fan!'

Which is your favourite ... team?
I'm a ... fan!
'Which is your favourite basketball team?' 'I'm a Chicago Bulls fan!'

Talk to your partner about your favourite sports. Practise the language above.

Grammar

Present Continuous (for the future)

We can use the Present Continuous to talk about future plans.
I'm playing volleyball *this afternoon.*
We aren't going to the sports centre tomorrow.
Are you coming to the match on Saturday?

Time expressions

this afternoon/evening
tomorrow/tonight
at the weekend
on Tuesday/Saturday/my birthday
at 4 o'clock
next week/month/year

What's Sally doing next week? Look at her diary and write complete sentences using the Present Continuous.

1 _____

2 _____

3 _____

4 _____

5 _____

APRIL	
Monday	Have riding lesson
Tuesday	Watch basketball match
Wednesday	Go swimming with Jenny
Thursday	Buy some new trainers
Friday	Go to Thai boxing class

Writing

Time Expressions: word order

A Put the words in the correct order.

1 ? / coming / this / sports centre / to / Mandy / evening / is / the

_____

2 week / are / Manchester United / next / playing

_____

3 ? / the / they / training / weekend / at / are

_____

4 moment / we / the / skating / at / are

_____

5 frozen waterfall / on / Jane / Saturday / climbing / is / a

_____

B Read the email. Find three mistakes with time expressions and correct them.

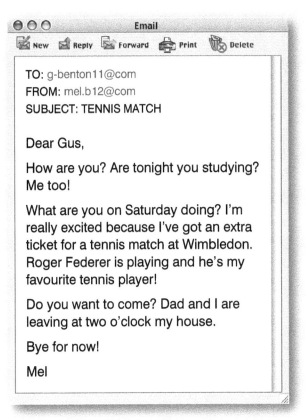

000 Email

New   Reply   Forward   Print   Delete

TO: g-benton11@com
FROM: mel.b12@com
SUBJECT: TENNIS MATCH

Dear Gus,

How are you? Are tonight you studying? Me too!

What are you on Saturday doing? I'm really excited because I've got an extra ticket for a tennis match at Wimbledon. Roger Federer is playing and he's my favourite tennis player!

Do you want to come? Dad and I are leaving at two o'clock my house.

Bye for now!

Mel

Task

C Write an email to a friend inviting him or her to a sports event. Use this plan to help you.

Begin like this:
Dear _____,

Paragraph 1
Ask how he/she is.
Ask what he/she is doing tonight.

Paragraph 2
Say why you are happy/excited.
Say what tickets you've got.
Say who is playing.

Paragraph 3
Invite your friend to come with you.
Say what time you are leaving.

Finish like this:
Bye for now!
_____ (your name)

D Read your email and check the word order.

8 People and Places

Quiz

What is this?

a The Great Towers of China
b The Great Gate of China
c The Great Wall of China

8 Lesson 1

🎧 **Listen and read.**

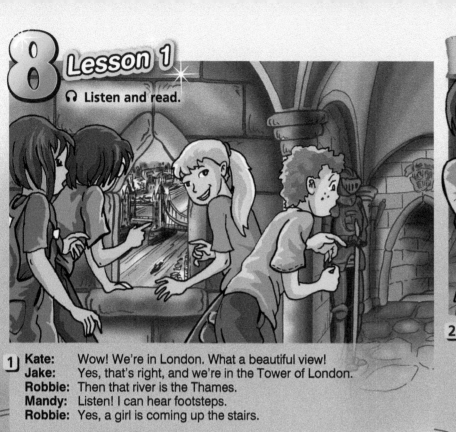

The Cortuga Mystery

1
Kate: Wow! We're in London. What a beautiful view!
Jake: Yes, that's right, and we're in the Tower of London.
Robbie: Then that river is the Thames.
Mandy: Listen! I can hear footsteps.
Robbie: Yes, a girl is coming up the stairs.

2
Sally: Hi, I'm Sally.
Jake: Hi! Do you live here?
Sally: No, but my dad works here.
Jake: How old is the tower?
Sally: It's 900 years old, I think.
Jake: Do people live here now?
Sally: Yes, the guards with their families and er ... a few ghosts!

3
Look at that knight!

It's holding a piece of the puzzle in its hand!

Oh, no! It's moving!

It's a ghost! Aaah!

4
Robbie: It isn't a ghost. It's me! I've got a piece of the puzzle!
Kate: Robbie! You and your stupid tricks!

5
Good work Robbie.

Be careful of the real ghosts, Sally.

Bye, Sally.

Vocabulary

Complete the sentences with these words.

> footsteps   ghosts   river   stairs   view

1 There are stories about _____ in this book!
2 The old man can't go up all these _____ .
3 There's a good _____ from the harbour.
4 Can you hear _____ outside? Who is it?
5 Can we swim in this _____?

Grammar

Present Simple and Present Continuous

We use the Present Simple for facts and habits.
I don't like cities!
Robbie often plays jokes on people.

We use the Present Continuous for actions that are happening now.
I'm wearing new jeans.

A   Circle the correct words.

1 People usually are visiting / visit the castle in summer.
2 Does / Is the Queen of England live in a castle?
3 Where's the guard? He is having / has lunch.
4 We never touch / are touching things in the museum.
5 Mick and Eddie clean / are cleaning their bedroom at the moment.
6 The baby doesn't play / isn't playing in the house now.

B   Complete the dialogue with the Present Simple or the Present Continuous of the verbs in brackets.

Bob: Hi Jane. It's Bob. I (1) _____ (call) from London. How are you?
Jane: I'm fine. Why are you in London?
Bob: Well, my mum usually (2) _____ (visit) my aunt at New Year.
Jane: But your aunt (3) _____ (not live) in London!
Bob: Yes, but this year my aunt (4) _____ (stay) with some friends in London for two weeks and so here we are.
Jane: (5) _____ (you have) fun?
Bob: Yes, London is fantastic!
Jane: I know and it's got amazing shops.
Bob: Yes, but I (6) _____ (not like) shopping.

Vocabulary

Match.

1 flat ☐
2 house ☐
3 castle ☐
4 houseboat ☐
5 cottage ☐
6 tower ☐
7 hut ☐
8 igloo ☐

Listening

🎧 **Listen to three children talking about their homes and complete the table.**

	Type of home:	Number of rooms:	View of:
Jill	(1) _____	(2) _____	(3) _____
Carl	(4) _____	(5) _____	(6) _____
Eve	(7) _____	(8) _____	(9) _____

Speaking

Talk about your home. Ask and answer these questions with your partner.

What kind of home is it?
Where is it?
How many rooms has it got?
Has it got a good view?
What can you see?
How many people live in it?

Writing

Write six sentences about your home. Answer the questions from the Speaking task.

Reading

Read the article. How many days a week do cowboys work?

Modern Cowboys

Cowboys wear cool clothes and ride horses. But what do they do? Dan Wood, an American cowboy, tells us about his job.

Dan gets up early – at 5 am! 'I sleep in a tent and it's very cold in the morning!' he says. First, he makes a fire and he cooks his breakfast. Then he must get on his horse and check his cows. That isn't easy – there are 4,000 cows!

'Sometimes the cows get sick and I give them medicine,' Dan says. 'And sometimes other animals kill them. Then I feel very sad.'

Dan mustn't stay in the same place for a long time. Cows eat a lot of grass, so Dan must find new areas with grass for them. Is it a hard job? 'Yes, it is. Cowboys work seven days a week and we don't make much money,' he says. 'But I love it!'

Guess what!
Horses don't usually lie down for a sleep. They stand up.

Comprehension

Answer the questions.

1 What time does Dan get up?
_____

2 Where does he sleep?
_____

3 What does Dan give sick cows?
_____

4 What must Dan find for the cows?
_____

5 Do cowboys make a lot of money?
_____

Vocabulary

Complete the phrases with these words.

cook	get	get on	get up	make

1 _____ early
2 _____ sick
3 _____ a horse
4 _____ a fire
5 _____ breakfast

Grammar

Must

We use must to talk about obligation. We use a bare infinitive after must.
I must clean the house.

Affirmative

I/You/He/She/It/We/They must go.

Negative

You/He/She/It/We/They mustn't (must not) go.

Question

Must I/you/he/she/it/we/they go?

Short answers

Yes, I/you/he/she/it/we/they must.
No, I/you/he/she/it/we/they mustn't.

Complete the sentences with must or mustn't.

1 Teachers _____ help their students.
2 _____ you study at weekends?
3 A good waiter _____ be calm.
4 Cowboys _____ get up early.
5 You _____ eat in the museum.
6 You're sick. You _____ go outside.
7 We _____ swim here. The sea isn't clean.
8 _____ she cook breakfast every day?

Vocabulary

Match.

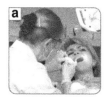

1 hairdresser
2 doctor
3 taxi driver
4 pilot
5 actor
6 dentist
7 shop assistant
8 firefighter

Listening

🎧 **Listen and write the numbers next to the jobs.**

a firefighter
b actor
c doctor
d shop assistant
e taxi driver

🎧 Sounds of English

A Complete the poem with these words.

phone   school   sea   wear

I don't want to do people's hair
Or sell them different clothes to (1) _____ .

I don't want to work in a (2) _____
Teaching kids about each rule.

I don't want to answer the (3) _____
In an office on my own.

I just want to sit by the (4) _____
With my friends, just them and me!

B Listen and check your answers.

Reading

Read the poster. Which place has got two names?

Welcome to Scotland!

Visit these fantastic places in Scotland!

Loch Ness

Loch Ness is a lake in Scotland. Some people say there's a monster in the lake! The monster's got a name – Nessie! They say it looks like a dinosaur. Thousands of people visit Loch Ness every year and they all want to see Nessie!

Glamis Castle

This big castle is hundreds of years old. There are many stories, secrets and mysteries about it. The Earls of Strathmore and Kinghorne live in the castle now, but it is also open for tourists.

Edinburgh

Edinburgh is the capital of Scotland. It's got many beautiful buildings and a castle. A lot of people visit Edinburgh in the summer for the Edinburgh Festival. Then you can watch plays, listen to music in the street and watch films. People call Edinburgh the 'Athens of the North' because there are buildings like the Parthenon on the Acropolis in Athens, Greece.

Comprehension

Complete the sentences with words from the poster.

1 The Loch Ness monster's name is _____ .
2 Glamis Castle is open for _____ .
3 There are a lot of beautiful _____ in Edinburgh.
4 There are _____, music and films at the Edinburgh Festival.
5 Another name for Edinburgh is _____ .

Say it like this!

Talking about places

What's it like?
It's big/small/fantastic.

What can you do there?
You can go shopping/to the park/to the beach.
You can visit museums.
You can see lots of interesting buildings.

Talk to your partner about your favourite town or city. Practise the language above.

Listening

🎧 **Answer the questions, then listen to check your answers.**

1 Where are the Pyramids?
  a India
  b Egypt
  c Spain

2 Which city is Euro Disney in?
  a London
  b Rome
  c Paris

3 The White House is in
  a Scotland.
  b the USA.
  c Australia.

4 Which city is the capital of Germany?
  a Berlin
  b Frankfurt
  c Bonn

5 What tells the time in London?
  a Little John
  b Big Brother
  c Big Ben

Speaking

Find five differences between the two pictures. Use the Present Continuous.

Writing

Connectors

A **Read about because and so.**

We use because to explain the reason for something.
I'm happy because it's Sunday.
We use so to explain the result of something.
It's the weekend, so we can play all day!

B **Complete the sentences with because or so.**

1 It's Saturday _____ we can go to the shops.
2 I don't like museums _____ they're boring!
3 Our house is big _____ I've got my own bedroom.
4 I like Tom's house _____ it's got a great view.
5 People visit Loch Ness _____ they want to see the monster.

C **Read the paragraph and complete the gaps with because or so.**

My Favourite Place

My favourite place in my town is the beach. It isn't a beautiful beach, but my friends and I have fun there. We don't usually swim there (1) _____ the sea is very cold! We sometimes play volleyball on the beach. There's also a café (2) _____ we often have lunch there. The view is great (3) _____ it's next to the sea.

Task ✏

D **Write a paragraph about your favourite place in your town or city. Use this plan to help you.**

Answer the questions.

What's your favourite place?

_____

What's it like?

_____

What do you do there?

_____

What other things are there in this place?

_____

E **Remember to use because and so to give reasons for things.**

Review 4

Vocabulary

A Find the stickers.

1	2
cycling	running

3	4
sailing	boxing

5	6
climbing	diving

7	8
ice-skating	riding

B Circle the correct words.

1 Taxi drivers have a strong / hard job.
2 Mum's sick. She must go to a doctor / medicine.
3 What are you doing? Get / Leave me alone!
4 The champion talks to his coach / knight every day.
5 The prize is a beautiful trophy / stair.
6 There are champions / ghosts in that old castle!
7 A famous coach practises / trains the football players.
8 The winner was very sad / calm after the race.

C Complete the word groups.

> cottage   hairdresser   kick
> lake   match   trophy

1 pilot, dentist, _____
2 flat, igloo, _____
3 competition, race, _____
4 sea, river, _____
5 boxer, footballer, _____
6 chase, push, _____

Grammar

A Complete the sentences with the Present Continuous of these verbs.

> eat feel make push ride run sleep watch

1 Angela _____ the ice skaters. ✔
2 The cowboy _____ sad. ✗
3 John and his dad _____ a fire. ✔
4 The children _____ in the park. ✗
5 Debbie _____ in her tent. ✔
6 I _____ a cow! ✗
7 He _____ the taxi down the road. ✔
8 This cow _____ flowers. ✗

B Put the words in the correct order.

1 ? / you / today / happy / feeling / are
   _____

2 ? / wearing / is / the cyclist / a helmet
   _____

3 ? / a / are / having / tomorrow / they / picnic
   _____

4 ? / for / Emma / practising / is / the race
   _____

5 ? / monster / swimming / lake / the / in / the / is
   _____

6 ? / living / a / houseboat / they / are / in
   _____

C Choose the correct answers.

1 We _____ to Scotland next week.
  a go
  b 're going

2 Look! That cat _____ a dog!
  a is chasing
  b chases

3 Neil always _____ our tennis matches.
  a wins
  b is winning

4 I _____ the flat every week.
  a 'm not cleaning
  b don't clean

5 Tim and Louise _____ at the moment.
  a don't train
  b aren't training

6 _____ Janet and Mike often get sick in winter?
  a Are
  b Do

7 'Where's your friend?' 'He _____ ready for the race.'
  a gets
  b 's getting

8 All my friends _____ a mountain tomorrow.
  a are climbing
  b climb

D Find the mistake in each sentence. Write the correct sentences.

1 You mustn't swimming in the river!
  _____

2 Champions must be train hard.
  _____

3 Cowboys sleep must in tents.
  _____

4 I must to cook breakfast today.
  _____

5 You must be not sad.
  _____

6 You must get up early every day?
  _____

7 She not must get up late.
  _____

8 Must students do their homework every day.
  _____

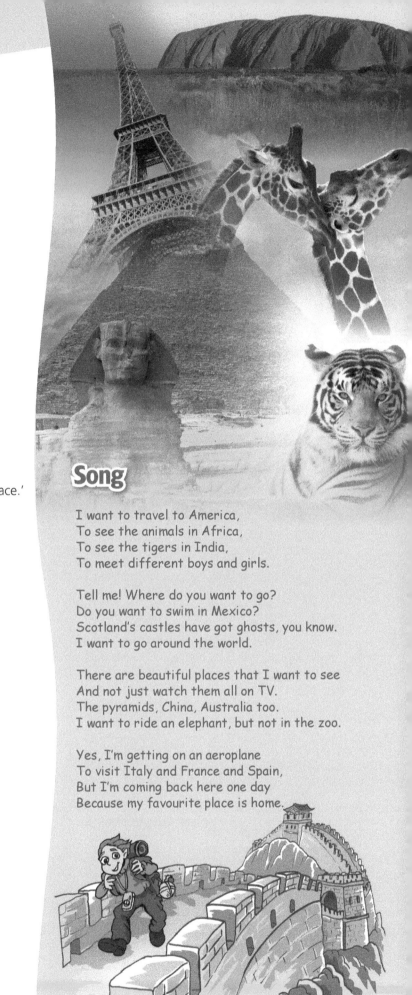

Song

I want to travel to America,
To see the animals in Africa,
To see the tigers in India,
To meet different boys and girls.

Tell me! Where do you want to go?
Do you want to swim in Mexico?
Scotland's castles have got ghosts, you know.
I want to go around the world.

There are beautiful places that I want to see
And not just watch them all on TV.
The pyramids, China, Australia too.
I want to ride an elephant, but not in the zoo.

Yes, I'm getting on an aeroplane
To visit Italy and France and Spain,
But I'm coming back here one day
Because my favourite place is home.

9 Holidays and Travel

Quiz

Where are the people?

a   on the sea
b   on a river
c   on a lake

Listen and read.

Excuse me? Can you help us?

Yes, of course. Come with us.

1)
Mandy: There's a lot of sand here. Are we on a beach?
Jake: No, we're in the middle of a desert. There's a pyramid behind you!
Kate: We're in Egypt. Its history is very interesting.
Robbie: It's very hot and I'm very thirsty!
Kate: I haven't got any water. I've only got some sun cream with me.
Robbie: Great! No, thanks.

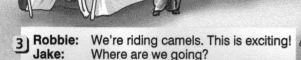

3)
Robbie: We're riding camels. This is exciting!
Jake: Where are we going?
Bedouin: We're going back to our camp. We were in the village for some things.
Mandy: The camels are very tall.
Kate: Be careful, Mandy!

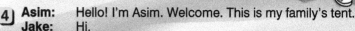

4)
Asim: Hello! I'm Asim. Welcome. This is my family's tent.
Jake: Hi.
Robbie: We're very thirsty.
Asim: Drink some of this! It's very good.
Robbie: Thanks. Mmm! That was delicious.
Kate: What was it?
Asim: Camel's milk.
Kate: Yuk!
Robbie: Come on, have some!
Kate: No, just some water for me.
Mandy: Oh, look at those beautiful goats.

5)
Mandy: Look at this! It's a piece of the puzzle.
Asim: It was in the desert. Do you want it?
Jake: Yes, please! It's very important to us.

6) Thanks, Asim.

The camel's milk was great!

Bye, Asim.

Vocabulary

Write the missing letters.

1 These are very big and very old buildings in Egypt. p _ _ _ _ _ _ _

2 This is a hot place with no trees, grass and not much water. d _ _ _ _ _ _

3 There is a lot of this on many beaches. s _ _ _

4 This is a small town. v _ _ _ _ _ _ _

5 This animal is tall and lives in Egypt and other hot countries. c _ _ _ _ _

Grammar

Past Simple - Be

We use the Past Simple to talk about events and habits in the past.
The food was delicious last night.
I was late for school every day.

Affirmative

I/he/she/it was
we/you/they were

Negative

I/he/she/it wasn't (was not)
we/you/they weren't (were not)

Question

Was I/he/she/it ...?
Were we/you/they ...?

Short answers

Yes, I/he/she/it was.   No, I/he/she/it wasn't.
Yes, we/you/they were.   No, we/you/they weren't.

Time Expressions

yesterday   two days/a month ago
last night/week/month   in July/2009

Note: The Past Simple of There is and There are is There was and There were.

Complete the dialogue with was, wasn't, were or weren't.

Girl: Where (1) _____ you last week? You (2) _____ at school all week. (3) _____ you sick?

Boy: Hey! What a lot of questions! No, I (4) _____. My family and I (5) _____ on holiday in the 'Sea of Sand'.

Girl: Is that a beach?

Boy: No. It's another name for the Sahara Desert.

Girl: Really? What (6) _____ it like?

Boy: It (7) _____ amazing. The Bedouin are very interesting people. There (8) _____ snakes, spiders and lizards in the desert.

Girl: (9) _____ it very hot?

Boy: Yes, it (10) _____, but only in the day. In the desert it's very cold at night.

Vocabulary

Match.

1 seat ☐
2 suitcase ☐
3 sun cream ☐
4 rucksack ☐
5 shorts ☐
6 tent ☐

Listening

🎧 **Listen and tick (✓) the correct picture.**

1 Which picture shows the hotel?

2 Where is the passport?

3 What does the girl's mother want to buy?

Speaking

Talk about your last holiday. Ask and answer these questions with your partner.

What kind of holiday was it?
Was the hotel good? What was it like?
Was the food nice? What was it?
Was the place beautiful? Why?
Were the people nice?

Writing

Write five sentences about your last holiday. Answer the questions in the Speaking task.

Up, up and away!

Reading

Read about hot air balloons. Who were the first passengers in a hot air balloon?

The Montgolfier brothers were from France and they were the inventors of the hot air balloon. They used smoke from a fire and filled a silk bag. Then they tied this bag to a basket. The brothers wanted to try their invention. They needed passengers, so they used a sheep, a duck and a chicken for the first flight of their hot air balloon. The hot air balloon stayed in the air for nine minutes!

The scientist Jean-François Pilatre de Rozier and his friend François Laurent travelled in a hot air balloon on 21st November, 1783. The King of France watched this flight too. The hot air balloon was up in the air for twenty minutes and then it landed in a field. Some farmers were scared of the hot air balloon.

Today hot air balloons are very popular because the view from them is always fantastic. A lot of people go for rides, and some people even get married in them!

Guess what!
The modern word 'pilot' comes from de Rozier's name Pilatre.

Comprehension

Write T (true) or F (false).

1 Three animals were the first passengers in a hot air balloon. ☐

2 The King of France was in the hot air balloon with de Rozier and Laurent. ☐

3 The hot air balloon stopped in a field. ☐

4 The farmers liked the hot air balloon. ☐

5 People go up in hot air balloons because they like the view. ☐

Vocabulary

Circle the correct words.

1 There was a lot of air / smoke because he started a fire.

2 All the passengers / farmers have got their tickets and passports.

3 We needed a basket / bottle of milk for breakfast.

4 The hot air balloon tied / landed in the park.

5 The flight / field from London to New York was seven hours long.

86

Grammar

Past Simple (regular verbs)

Affirmative

We use the Past Simple to talk about events and habits in the past. We add -ed to regular verbs in the Past Simple.
He worked in a hotel two years ago.

Spelling rules

dance   danced
try   tried
stop   stopped

A Look back at the text. How many regular Past Simple verbs can you find?

B Complete the paragraph with the Past Simple of the verbs in brackets.

Jack (1) _____ (live) with the Donald family, but he (2) _____ (want) to see the world. One Saturday morning, he (3) _____ (carry) all his toys inside. Then he (4) _____ (walk) down the street and he (5) _____ (chase) the cat from next door. It was a nice day, so he (6) _____ (stop) at the park. He (7) _____ (watch) a football match, but then he was hungry. Mrs Donald (8) _____ (cook) chicken on Saturday. It's his favourite food. So Jack is at home now. Who is Jack? Guess what! He's a cat!

Vocabulary

A Match.

1 bus ☐
2 plane ☐
3 train ☐
4 ship ☐

B Circle the correct words.

1 You can get a plane at a(n) port / airport.

2 Lots of people are on the stop / platform because the train is late.

3 There are trains and buses at stations / platforms.

4 The ship is coming into the port / station.

5 They're waiting at a bus port / stop.

Listening

🎧 **Where are these people? Listen to the conversations and number the places 1-5.**

a   at an airport ☐

b   at a train station ☐

c   in a car ☐

d   at a bus stop ☐

e   on a ship ☐

🎧 Sounds of English

A Read these verbs in the Past Simple tense. How do you say the -ed part of each verb? Listen to check.

1 wanted
2 liked
3 stopped

B Read these verbs aloud. Which sound do they end in, id or t?

looked ☐   watched ☐

needed ☐   visited ☐

worked ☐   touched ☐

Song

We love holidays. Everybody loves holidays.
At Christmas, at Easter, in summer too,
We can all do what we want to do.

We went skiing last Christmas. It was really good fun.
We played in the snow under the winter sun.
We called our parents on the telephone,
'It's fantastic here. We don't want to come home.'

We had a long summer holiday by the sea.
I loved swimming with my family.
In June, July and August. That was really cool.
We were back in September to get ready for school.

Cool Holidays!

Reading

Read about two different kinds of holiday. Which of the holidays do you like?

Holly, 10

Rick, 12

I went on holiday to New York with my family last year. We went by plane and we stayed in a hotel in the city centre. The shops in New York are great, but some were very expensive! I bought three pairs of jeans! They were cheap. I ate lots of burgers and French fries. One evening we saw a play at a theatre on Broadway. It was exciting because there was a famous actor in it!

We had a great holiday in France last summer. We travelled by car, but we took our bikes with us. Every day we went swimming and cycling. We visited some very interesting museums and we ate at some fantastic restaurants. French food is delicious. At night we slept in tents. We had two tents – one for my mum and dad and one for me and my sister. My sister told me stories every night. Sometimes I was very scared!

Comprehension

Complete the table.

	Rick	Holly
Place:	(1) _____	(2) _____
Travelled:	(3) _____	(4) _____
Stayed in:	(5) _____	(6) _____

Say it like this!

Talking about travel

How do you get to ...?
by car/bike/bus/train/taxi
on foot
How do you get to school?
I go by bus.

Talk to your partner about how you get to these places. Practise the language above.

the beach
your friend's house

the park
the shops

Grammar

Past Simple (irregular verbs)

Affirmative

We do not add –ed to the Past Simple affirmative of irregular verbs. They change in different ways. See page 126 for a list of irregular verbs.

They went on holiday to the USA last year.
He wore shorts last summer.

Complete the dialogue with the Past Simple of these verbs.

buy eat go have swim wear

Ellie: How was your summer, Sarah?
Sarah: Fantastic! We (1) _____ to Mykonos.
Ellie: Wow! Was it hot?
Sarah: Yes, it was. We (2) _____ a great time.
Ellie: Were the beaches nice?
Sarah: Yes! We (3) _____ in the sea every morning, and I (4) _____ my new T-shirt.
Ellie: What about the food?
Sarah: It was delicious, and very cheap. We (5) _____ in a different restaurant every night. We also (6) _____ some beautiful things from the shops.
Ellie: You were very lucky.

Writing

Adjectives

A Read about how we use adjectives.

We use adjectives to describe nouns. We can use them before a noun or after the verb be.
There is a beautiful beach near here.
The beach is beautiful.

B Put the words in the correct order.

1 hotel / stayed / nice / a / we / in

_____

2 expensive / were / the / very / shops

_____

3 city / Rome / a / is / fantastic

_____

4 wasn't / food / the / good / very

_____

5 meal / in the café / a / had / we / delicious

_____

C Complete Emily's postcard with these adjectives.

beautiful   delicious   difficult interesting   special

Dear Joe,

I'm having a great time in Amsterdam! It's a city with a very (1) _____ history. There are a lot of (2) _____ buildings and parks. Yesterday we cycled around the city centre. It wasn't (3) _____ because Amsterdam has got (4) _____ roads for bikes! This morning we had breakfast at a café near our hotel. The food was (5) _____!

See you soon!

Emily

Task

D Think about a city you know. Write a postcard to a friend. Use this plan to help you.

Begin like this:
Dear _____,

Complete the sentences:
I'm having a great time in _____ .
The city is very _____ .
The city has got _____ .
There are (a lot of) _____
_____ .

Yesterday, I/we _____
_____ .

Last night/This morning, I/we _____
_____ .

Finish like this:
See you soon!
_____ (your name)

E Remember to use adjectives to describe nouns.

10 Fame!

The Cortuga Mystery

Listen and read.

1

Where are we? Is this a concert?

We're in a film studio!

There's a director and a cameraman over there.

2
Director: Cut! Who are you?
Kate: Sorry! Are you shooting a film?
Director: Yes. Now, go and put on your costume.
Kate: But ...
Director: You've got a role in the film. You're Debbie. Go to the dressing room now, please!

Later ...

3
Did you learn your lines?

Yes, I did. It wasn't difficult. I only say, 'Dinner is ready, Sir.'

OK. Let's start! All actors please come to the set.

4
Kate's got talent. She didn't say a lot, but she was great!

Yes, she's also clever and pretty.

And famous now!

5
Robbie: Can I have your autograph?
Kate: Very funny! But I can give you this!
Jake: It's the last piece of the puzzle! Where was it?
Kate: The director gave me this beautiful bag because he liked my acting. The piece was in the bag.
Mandy: Well done, Debbie! Er ... sorry, Kate.

6
Let's go home now!

Hurray! Now we can do the puzzle.

Vocabulary

Complete the sentences with these words.

> autograph cameraman director role set

1 The _____ is shooting a part of the film.
2 I didn't want a _____ in the play so the teacher gave it to Mary.
3 Spielberg is famous because he was the _____ of films like *Jurassic Park*.
4 I got my favourite actor's _____ last week.
5 The actors are on the _____ now.

Grammar

Negative

I/you/he/she/it/we/they didn't go
The singer didn't give any autographs.

Questions

Did I/you/he/she/it/we/they go ...?
Did you see the new film?

Short answers

Yes, I/you/he/she/it/we/they did.
No, I/you/he/she/it/we/they didn't.
Did he go to the concert? Yes, he did.

Complete the dialogue with the Past Simple of the verbs in brackets.

Ellie: (1) _____ (you/buy) the tickets for the Girlzone concert?
Steve: No, (2) I _____ .
Ellie: Why not?
Steve: Well, I went to the music shop at 5 o'clock and they (3) _____ (not/have) any tickets.
Ellie: (4) _____ (they/sell) them all?
Steve: Yes!
Ellie: Oh, no! I really wanted to go to that concert!
Steve: Me too! But listen to this. I was outside the music shop and I saw Jodie from the band!
Ellie: Wow! (5) _____ (you/speak) to her?
Steve: Yes, I (6) _____ . I asked for her autograph.
Ellie: And?
Steve: She (7) _____ (not/give) me her autograph, but she gave me these.
Ellie: What are they?
Steve: Two free tickets for the concert!
Ellie: Oh, Steve! That's fantastic!

Vocabulary

Match.

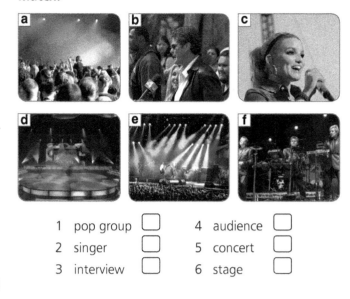

1 pop group ☐   4 audience ☐
2 singer ☐   5 concert ☐
3 interview ☐   6 stage ☐

Listening

🎧 **Do the quiz, then listen and check your answers.**

1 Where is Kylie Minogue from?
   a Australia   b England   c the USA
2 Robbie Williams sang in the pop group
   a 'Boyzone'.   b 'Take That'.   c 'Steps'.
3 Who sang the song 'Baby one more time'?
   a Madonna   b Christina Aguilera   c Britney Spears
4 Greece won the Eurovision Song Contest in
   a 2004.   b 2005.   c 2006.
5 One of the singers in the pop group *Destiny's Child* was
   a Beyonce.   b Avril Lavigne.   c Shakira.

Speaking

Play 'Guess the star'. Ask your partner questions and guess who your partner's star is! Then think of a star and answer your partner's questions about him/her.

Is it a man/woman?
Is he/she from England/USA/Egypt
Does he/sing act/sing/play a sport?
Was he/she ...?
Did he/she ...?

Writing

Write five sentences about the star you thought of in the Speaking task.

Reading

Read about Walt Disney. What was Walt Disney's dream?

Who was Walt Disney?

Walt Disney is famous all over the world for his films. He won 26 Oscars and this is a world record. Some of his cartoon characters, like Mickey Mouse and Donald Duck, are now very old! Mickey's date of 'birth' is 18th November, 1928!

What do we know about his early life?

Walt was born in 1901 in Chicago in the USA. His family was poor but because Walt drew fantastic pictures, he sold some to neighbours and made some money. (1) _____

How did he start making films?

Walt started his first film company at twenty-one, but it didn't make any money. (2) _____ He had a little money so he and his brother started a small film company in their uncle's garage! (3) _____ Later they moved to a big studio and they made long films like *Snow White and the Seven Dwarfs*, *Dumbo*, *Pinocchio* and *Bambi*.

When did Disneyland® open?

Walt Disney always wanted to open his own amusement park. It was his dream. (4) _____ Children and adults loved it and soon it had visitors from all over the world. (5) _____

Guess what!
Mickey Mouse's name was 'Mortimer' at first, but Walt Disney's wife didn't like it and changed it to Mickey!

Comprehension

Complete the article with these sentences.

a   In 1955 his Disneyland® opened in Florida.

b   First they made short films.

c   He loved drawing animals.

d   There are also Disneyland® Parks in other countries like France and Japan.

e   He then decided to go to Hollywood because his brother lived there.

Vocabulary

Write the missing letters.

1   This is a person or animal in a film or book.   c _ _ _ _ _ _ _ _

2   This is something you want very much and think about a lot.   d _ _ _ _ _

3   You keep your car in this.   g _ _ _ _ _ _

4   They live in the house near you.   n _ _ _ _ _ _ _ _ _ _

5   People with only a little money are this.   p _ _ _ _

Grammar

Wh- questions in the Past Simple

We can use Wh- questions with the Past Simple to find out more information about an action in the past.
Which film star did you see?
Who did you see?
Where did you see him?
When did you see him?
Why did he speak to you?
What did he say?
How did you feel?
Whose autograph did you get?

Note: When the question word asks about the subject (person, animal or thing) then the verb stays in the affirmative form.
Who went to the cinema?

A Put the words in the correct order to make questions.

1 did / your neighbours / Disneyland / go / when / to
_____?

2 that / Mickey Mouse T-shirt / you / where / buy / did
_____?

3 say / the interview / did / in / Jim Carrey / what
_____?

4 last night / film / which / see / they / did
_____?

5 Nancy / why / him / did / give / the tickets
_____?

6 interview / the reporter / did / who / in the film
_____?

B Write questions in the Past Simple about the underlined words. Use these question words.

> how   what   when   where   who   whose

1 <u>Jack and his sister</u> came to the studio.
_____?

2 I got the singer's autograph <u>last week</u>.
_____?

3 The film star arrived <u>by car</u>.
_____?

4 He saw me <u>at the concert</u>.
_____?

5 They had <u>free tickets for the concert</u>.
_____?

6 That was <u>Shakira's</u> interview on TV.
_____?

Vocabulary

Match.

1 adventure film ☐
2 cartoon ☐
3 comedy ☐
4 drama ☐
5 musical ☐
6 science fiction ☐

Listening

🎧 **Listen to two friends talking in a DVD shop and tick the DVDs they choose.**

1 a drama ☐
2 a science fiction film ☐
3 a comedy ☐
4 a musical ☐
5 an adventure film ☐

🎧 Sounds of English

A Read these pairs of words. What is the difference between the sounds of the coloured letters in each pair? Listen and check.

1 dance, cartoon
2 go, stage
3 was, small
4 scary, you

B Now listen and write the missing letters.

1 ea __ y
2 __ omed __
3 __ ara __ e
4 funn __
5 ex __ iting
6 __ leep
7 __ oun __
8 pie __ e

Reading

Read the interview with Zoe.
What did Zoe do at the audition?

Lessons in Fame

Do you want to be famous? This is Zoe Gregory's dream. She tells us about life at the Elmfield School of Drama.

Interviewer: Why did you want to go to a school for drama, Zoe?

Zoe: Well, I always wanted to become a star one day. At this school we have normal lessons, but we also have singing and acting lessons. We often stay at school after lessons because we must practise.

Interviewer: When did you start lessons at Elmfield?

Zoe: Last year. I was eleven then.

Interviewer: Did you have an audition?

Zoe: Yes. It was difficult because the school only takes a few new pupils every year.

Interviewer: What did you do at the audition?

Zoe: I sang a song from the musical *Annie*.

Interviewer: Did you feel nervous?

Zoe: Yes, I did! Now I don't usually get very nervous. I try and relax before I go on stage. It's strange but famous stars often feel nervous too!

Interviewer: Do you enjoy school life at Elmfield?

Zoe: Yes, very much! It's hard work, but I'm very lucky. This is a great school.

Comprehension

Answer the questions.

1 What special subjects does Zoe learn?

_____

2 How many new pupils does Elmfield School take every year?

_____

3 How old is Zoe now?

_____

4 When did Zoe sing a song from the musical *Annie*?

_____

5 What does Zoe say about stars?

_____

Say it like this!

Talking about stars

Who's your favourite ...?
I'm crazy about ... . He's/She's a/an fantastic/ amazing/great ...!
Who's your favourite actor?
I'm crazy about Orlando Bloom. He's a fantastic actor!

Talk to your partner about your favourite stars. Practise the language above.

Listening

🎧 **Listen to a discussion about two children's auditions for a TV programme called *Young Stars* and complete the table.**

Name:	Amber	Damian
Age:	(1) _____	(4) _____
Talent:	(2) _____	(5) _____
Score:	(3) _____	(6) _____

Speaking

Read the dialogue with your partner. Then change the red words to make your own dialogue. Practise it with your partner.

Amy: Did you see the film *Pirates of the Caribbean* on TV last night?

Jack: Yes, it was good.

Amy: Orlando Bloom is my favourite actor because he's got a lot of talent.

Jack: I don't like him. I'm crazy about Johnny Depp. He's a great actor.

Amy: I saw an interview with him and he was really interesting.

Writing

Using paragraphs

A Read about how we use paragraphs.

We usually separate a piece of writing into different parts, called paragraphs.

A paragraph is usually two or more sentences.

Each paragraph has a different subject.

The first sentence of a paragraph usually introduces the topic.

B Read these three sentences from the first paragraph of a film review. Which order do they go in? Write 1, 2 or 3.

My parents enjoyed it too. ☐

It was a cartoon, but it wasn't just for children. ☐

The film *Shrek* was fantastic. ☐

C Now read the rest of the film review. What are the topics of these two paragraphs?

The story was about a monster, Shrek, and a beautiful princess, Fiona. Fiona didn't want to marry the handsome prince. She liked Shrek!

The character of Shrek was great and I also liked his friend, Donkey. Their jokes were very funny!

Task ✏️

D Write a review of a film. Use this plan to help you.

Answer the questions.

Paragraph 1
What was the film like?

_____

What kind of film was it?

_____

Paragraph 2
What was the story about?

_____

_____

Paragraph 3
Which characters did you like?

_____

Why?

_____

Remember to separate your review into paragraphs.

Review 5

Vocabulary

A Match.

1 sun   a group
2 bus   b film
3 pop   c cream
4 hot air   d room
5 science fiction   e balloon
6 dressing   f stop

B Circle the odd one out.

1 passenger   actor   star
2 drama   seat   comedy
3 director   concert   film
4 hotel   train   plane
5 sheep   camel   camp

C Find the stickers.

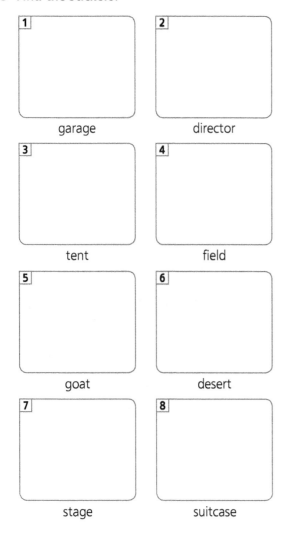

1	2
garage	director
3	4
tent	field
5	6
goat	desert
7	8
stage	suitcase

D Circle the correct words.

1 Bill hasn't got any money. He's poor / nervous.
2 The history of film is very expensive / interesting.
3 Pilots work on planes / ships.
4 Can I have your audience / autograph please?
5 Karen is our neighbour / fan. She lives next to us.
6 Have you got any bus passports / tickets?

Grammar

A Complete the postcard with the Past Simple of the verbs in brackets.

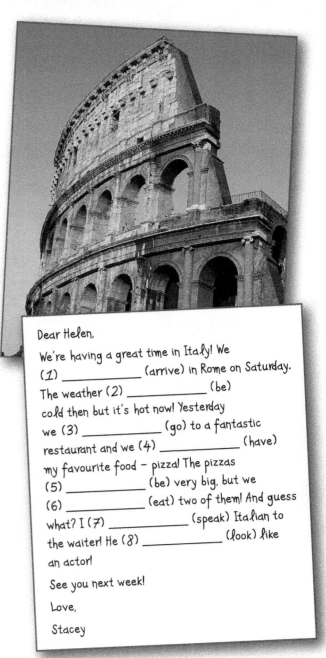

Dear Helen,

We're having a great time in Italy! We
(1) _____ (arrive) in Rome on Saturday.
The weather (2) _____ (be)
cold then but it's hot now! Yesterday
we (3) _____ (go) to a fantastic
restaurant and we (4) _____ (have)
my favourite food – pizza! The pizzas
(5) _____ (be) very big, but we
(6) _____ (eat) two of them! And guess
what? I (7) _____ (speak) Italian to
the waiter! He (8) _____ (look) like
an actor!

See you next week!

Love,

Stacey

B **Write the sentences with the negative form of the Past Simple.**

1 The hot air balloon was expensive.

   _____

2 The hotel had a swimming pool.

   _____

3 We liked the concert.

   _____

4 The brothers were inventors.

   _____

5 The baby ate my ice cream.

   _____

6 I wore my new T-shirt at the beach.

   _____

C **Use these words to make questions in the Past Simple. Then complete the short answers.**

1 Cindy / go / to Paris?

   _____

   Yes, _____ .

2 Mark and Chris / buy / a new tent?

   _____

   No, _____ .

3 you / ride / a camel / in the desert?

   _____

   Yes, _____ .

4 your dad / meet / a famous actor?

   _____

   No, _____ .

5 You and Jane / get / a role / in the play?

   _____

   Yes, _____ .

D **Look at the answers and write the correct question words.**

1 '_____ did the train leave?' 'At 1.30 pm.'

2 '_____ film did they see?' 'Ratatouille.'

3 '_____ did Anna go on holiday?' 'To Spain.'

4 '_____ did John go to London?' 'By car.'

5 '_____ did you get that star's autograph?'
  'Because he's famous.'

6 '_____ passport is this?' 'It's my brother's.'

Song

Please! Please! Can I have your autograph?
Please! Please! Can I take your photograph?
Every day I must smile and laugh.
This is my life. I'm a superstar.

Please! Please! Can you give me an interview?
Please! Please! Talk to me. Is it really true?
Where did you go? What did you do?
There are always questions for a superstar.

Fame! Fame! I always wanted fame.
Fame! Fame! Everybody knows my name.

Yes! Yes! I am working in the studio.
Yes! Yes! The director is ready to go.
What do you think of my new video?
This is my life. I'm a superstar.

Quiz

What's a young cheetah called?

a   puppy
b   teddy bear
c   cub

🎧 **Listen and read.**

1)

Jake:	We're back in Uncle Oliver's house!
Robbie:	That's strange! It's still 10th July.
Mandy:	And Henry's in the same place.
Kate:	Yes, but let's do the puzzle. We've got all the pieces now.
Jake:	Please do it, Mandy. You're better at puzzles than us!

2)

Mandy:	Look. It's a map and it shows a path to a cave.
Kate:	Oh no! Caves are full of horrible bats.
Robbie:	Don't worry, Kate, they're not dangerous. Sharks are more dangerous than bats, Kate.
Kate:	Very funny, Robbie!
Jake:	Look! This cave is near Eagle Rock! It's a beautiful place with butterflies and birds.
Mandy:	Well, butterflies are nicer than bats!

3)

Robbie:	Are we ready?
Kate:	Yes, we've got a torch, binoculars and a map of Cortuga!
Jake:	Good! We need some food. I can make some sandwiches.
Robbie:	What do lizards eat?
Mandy:	Insects and worms. Uncle Oliver keeps some here.
Robbie:	That's cool. Here, Henry, eat a worm!

4)

I'm tired. Are we nearly there?

Let's stop for a few minutes.

OK, but look up there! There's an eagle in the sky!

We're near Eagle Point. Now where's the cave?

Vocabulary

Circle the correct word(s).

1 It's dark in here. We need a torch / some binoculars.
2 Bats / Worms usually live in caves and fly at night.
3 A long time ago people lived in paths / caves.
4 Butterflies are small insects / maps.
5 I'm dangerous / tired. I'm going to bed!

Grammar

Comparative

We use the comparative form to compare two people, animals or things. We often use the word *than* after the comparative form.
Jake is taller than Mandy.

Short adjectives

tall	taller
nice	nicer
big	bigger
pretty	prettier

Long adjectives

beautiful	more beautiful

Irregular adjectives

good	better
bad	worse
many/much	more

Complete the sentences with the comparative form of the adjectives in brackets.

1 Bats are _____ (ugly) than butterflies.
2 Insects are _____ (small) than birds.
3 Cats are _____ (good) than lizards.
4 Camels are _____ (tall) than lions.
5 Sharks are _____ (dangerous) than cows.

Vocabulary

Match.

1 dolphin ☐
2 eagle ☐
3 leopard ☐
4 swan ☐
5 whale ☐
6 worm ☐

Listening

🎧 **Listen to someone talking about crocodiles and complete the fact sheet.**

Crocodile Facts

Size: can be (1) _____ metres long
Eats: a lot of (2) _____, birds, snakes and big animals like zebras and (3) _____
Country: (4) _____, India, America, Africa
Lives in: the sea, (5) _____ and lakes
Lives for: up to (6) _____ years

Speaking

Talk to your partner and compare these animals. Use these words to help you.

beautiful big clever dangerous
short small strong ugly

Writing

Write five sentences about your favourite animal. Answer these questions.

What is your favourite animal?
What colour is it?
What does it eat?
Where does it live?
What can it do?

Reading

Read about some presidents' pets. How did the pony get up to Archie Roosevelt's bedroom?

Presidents' Pets

A lot of presidents of the USA love animals! The most popular pets for presidents are dogs and the Obamas have a Portuguese Water Dog called Bo.

President Clinton's daughter, Chelsea, had a black and white cat called Socks. He was the most famous cat in the world while he lived at the White House.

George W. Bush had the most unusual pet - a longhorn cow called Ofelia. The cow lived at his farm in Texas.

Theodore Roosevelt had the most pets of all presidents. His six children had many pets! One day Roosevelt's son, Archie, was sick and his brother Quentin brought him a visitor - his pet pony! He put the pony in the lift at the White House and took it up to Archie's bedroom! Another time Quentin also put some snakes on his father's desk!

John F. Kennedy also had many pets. His daughter, Caroline, had a pony called Macaroni. This pony was very popular and it got letters from fans!

Sometimes presidents get presents from other countries. The most unusual present was from the King of Siam. It was some elephants!

This is Mount Rushmore and it has got the largest sculpture in the world. From left to right presidents of the USA: George Washington, Thomas Jefferson, Theodore Roosevelt and Abraham Lincoln.

Guess what! 75% of American families have a pet. There are 77 million cats in the USA!

Comprehension

Circle the correct words.

1 President Obama's daughters have a dog / cat.
2 Quentin / Archie Roosevelt brought a big animal into the White House.
3 Fans sent letters to Caroline / Macaroni.
4 Quentin put snakes on the president's / his brother's desk.
5 One President of the USA gave / got a strange gift.

Vocabulary

Complete the sentences with these words.

important   lift   president   popular   unusual

1 The actor gets lots of letters because he is _____ .
2 Don't walk up the stairs. Take the _____!
3 Bill Clinton was a _____ of the USA.
4 You must read this message, it's _____!
5 That's a(n) _____ bird. What is it?

Grammar

Superlative

We use the superlative form to compare a person, an animal or thing with many other people, animals or things. *Polly is the nicest cat in the world!*

Short adjectives

tall	the tallest
big	the biggest
nice	the nicest
pretty	the prettiest

Long adjectives

interesting	the most interesting
horrible	the most horrible

Irregular adjectives

good	the best
bad	the worst
many/much	the most

Write sentences about these animals. Use the superlative form.

1 the shark / has got / ugly / face

_____

2 the elephant / is / big / animal

_____

3 the bird / has got / beautiful colours

_____

4 the shark / is / good / swimmer

_____

5 the bird / is / small / animal

_____

Vocabulary

Match.

a

b

c

1	goldfish ☐
2	kitten ☐
3	parrot ☐
4	pony ☐
5	puppy ☐
6	rabbit ☐

d

e

f

Listening

🎧 **Listen and write T (true) or F (false).**

1 Lucy likes mice. ☐

2 Lucy's dad thinks rabbits are good pets. ☐

3 Lucy's mum doesn't like cats. ☐

4 Lucy's brother has got a goldfish. ☐

5 Lucy's dad buys her a pet. ☐

🎧 **Sounds of English**

A Read these words aloud, paying attention to the sounds of the letters in red. What are the two different sounds?

1	animal	4	love
2	fun	5	parrot
3	bat	6	puppy

B Now put the words in A in the correct columns. Then listen and check your answers.

monkey	rabbit
1 _____	4 _____
2 _____	5 _____
3 _____	6 _____

Song

She's the nicest. She's the prettiest.
She's the most interesting of them all.
She's the best girl in the world.
And she comes to me when I call.
She dances to the music.
She loves to run and to play.
She's the cleverest, the most beautiful.
And I take her out every day.

She's my pet and I love her.
And I know she's my best friend.
She's better than any other.
Oh! Look! She's in her basket again!

She's never naughty. She's always good,
Because I taught her what to do.
She's got lovely eyes. She chases butterflies,
And she always eats her food.

She's my pet and I love her.
Now she wants to go out again.
She's my dog. My little Susie.
And she knows she's my best friend.

My Clever Pet!

Read about three clever animals. Which animal do you think is the cleverest?

Lynn, 10, England

Our parrot, Arthur, is the cleverest bird in the world! He can talk and he can also count to five now. My mum taught him, and it was hard work. My parrot can say lots of words, but his favourite words are 'What's for dinner?' He's always very hungry!

Helen, 9, Greece

My cat, Nelly, is nicer and cleverer than a dog! I found her in the street. She was a hungry sick kitten, so I took her home. My parents weren't very happy about that at first, but now they like her very much. Nelly's favourite person in our family is Mum because she gives nice food to Nelly.

Alvin, 12, USA

Our dog, Mattie, is the best pet in the world. He can do clever tricks, but sometimes he's very naughty! One day he chased another dog in the park and we lost him. We looked all around the neighbourhood for him, but we didn't find him. We were very sad and we went home. Who was outside our front door? Our dog, Mattie!

Comprehension

Complete the table.

	LYNN	HELEN	ALVIN
Name:	(1) _____	(4) _____	(7) _____
Animal:	(2) _____	(5) _____	(8) _____
Can:	(3) _____, _____	(6) _____	(9) _____

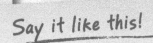

Say it like this!

Talking about animals

What a/an + adjective + noun!
What a beautiful horse!

Talk to your partner about these animals. Practise the language above.

Grammar

We use comparatives to compare two people, animals or things.
Jenny's pet is better than your pet.
Spiders are smaller than elephants.

We use superlatives to compare one person, animal or thing with many others.
Cats are the best pets for families.
Parrots are the most beautiful pets in the world.

Complete the paragraph with the comparative or superlative forms of the adjectives in brackets.

Komodo Dragons

The Komodo dragon is one of (1) _____ (scary) animals in the world! They are lizards, but they are (2) _____ (big) and (3) _____ (dangerous) than other lizards. Some of them are more than 3 metres long! Komodo dragons have got lots of teeth and they are (4) _____ (fast) than many other animals. They only eat meat. Komodo dragons live on some islands in Indonesia. They also live in zoos and they are one of the (5) _____ (popular) animals there. Visitors find them amazing.

Writing

Spelling

A Put the letters in the correct order to spell animal words from this unit.

1 g e l a e   _____
2 t f u y b l t e r   _____
3 l i c o r d c o e   _____
4 l e w a h   _____
5 o r l d e a p   _____

B Read the advert. There are five spelling mistakes in it. Can you find them and correct them?

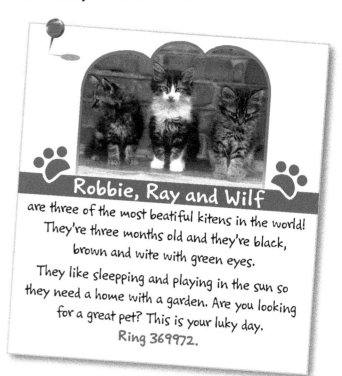

Robbie, Ray and Wilf

are three of the most beatiful kitens in the world! They're three months old and they're black, brown and wite with green eyes. They like sleeping and playing in the sun so they need a home with a garden. Are you looking for a great pet? This is your luky day. Ring 369972.

Task

C Choose one of the photos below and write your own advert for it. Use this plan to help you.

Answer the questions.

What are their names?
_____

What kind of animals are they?
_____

How old are they?
_____

What do they look like?
_____

What do they like doing?
_____

What do they need?
_____

D Read your advert and check your spelling carefully.

12 Weather and Nature

Quiz

What are these lights called?

a flashes

b lightning

c lamps

The Cortuga Mystery

🎧 Listen and read.

1
Kate: Look at the clouds! It's going to rain.
Mandy: And we haven't got any raincoats! We're going to get wet.
Jake: This is it! We're at Eagle Point.
Robbie: Come on. The cave's over there.

2
Mandy: I can't see you. Where are you?
Kate: Switch on the torch, Robbie.
Robbie: What are we looking for?
Jake: I don't know ... Let's look around.

3
It's a gold box! Jake, open it!

4
Kate: Listen! Footsteps! Who is it?
Oliver: It's me. Well done, children!
Jake: Uncle Oliver! What are you doing here?
Oliver: I saw the puzzle at home. This is the lost medallion of Sethenca. I must take it to the museum. How did you find the missing pieces?
Robbie: It's a long story!
Oliver: OK. You can tell me all about it at home.

5
Look! It isn't raining anymore.

And there's a beautiful rainbow in the sky.

We're going to have a great summer now!

Yes, but no more adventures, I hope!

Vocabulary

Circle the correct words.

1 There are many different colours in a cloud / rainbow.
2 Can you switch on / open the TV? My favourite show is on.
3 We need medallions / raincoats. We mustn't get wet.
4 Don't swim near the boxes / rocks – it's dangerous!
5 We're seeing / looking for a cave, but we can't find it.

Grammar

Be going to

We use be going to:
a to talk about future plans and intentions.
   He's going to look at the map.
b to predict that something will happen when we have some proof or information.
   Look at the clouds. It's going to rain.
We use a bare infinitive after be going to.
Donna's going to play outside.

Affirmative

I'm (I am) going to play.
You're (You are) going to play.
He's/She's/It's (He/She/It is) going to play.
We're/You're/They're (We/You/They are) going to play.

Negative

I'm not (I am not) going to play.
You aren't (are not) going to play.
He/She/It isn't (is not) going to play.
We/You/They aren't (are not) going to play.

Questions

Am I going to play?
Are you going to play?
Is he/she/it going to play?
Are we/you/they going to play?

Short Answers

Yes, I am. / No, I'm not.
Yes, you are. / No, you aren't.
Yes, he/she/it is. / No, he/she/it isn't.
Yes, we/you/they are. / No, we/you/they aren't.

Time expressions

tomorrow, in the morning, this weekend/summer/evening
next week/month/year, in a week/month/year

Complete the dialogue with the correct form of be going to and the verbs in brackets.

Ricky: (1) _____ you _____ (go) on holiday?
Mark: No, I (2) _____ . I (3) _____ (stay) at home.
Ricky: What (4) _____ you _____ (do)?
Mark: We (5) _____ (make) a tree house!
Ricky: On your own?
Mark: No, my dad (6) _____ (help) us. Then we (7) _____ (invite) all our friends there. You can come too.

Vocabulary

Match.

1 rainy ☐
2 sunny ☐
3 cloudy ☐
4 snowy ☐
5 windy ☐
6 foggy ☐

Listening

🎧 **Listen and write the numbers next to the weather symbols. There is one extra symbol that you do not need to use.**

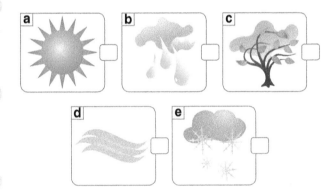

Speaking

Talk about your plans for this weekend with your partner. Ask and answer these questions.

Is it going to be rainy/sunny?
What are you going to wear?
What are you going to eat?
Where are you going to go?
Who are you going to see?

Writing

Write five sentences about your plans for this weekend. Answer the questions in the Speaking task.

Nature in DANGER

AFRICA

Reading

Read the text. Where does the journey finish?

It's September and a team of scientists is going to start a journey of 2,000 kilometres through the rainforest in the Congo, Africa. This is the second largest rainforest in the world and there are thousands of kinds of plants and animals there.

The scientists will travel on foot because there are no roads. They will carry clothes, food and tents in their rucksacks. What will they find in the rainforests? Will they survive this dangerous journey? Why are they making this journey?

'Companies want to cut down the trees so they can sell them as wood. This will be very bad for the animals and plants,' says the leader of the group, Dr Michael Fay. He's going to write lots of information about the rainforest. He wants to show us a very important thing. We mustn't destroy this rainforest because it is one of the last wild places on Earth.

More than a year later, the team arrives at the Atlantic Ocean. This is the end of their amazing journey. It was hard, but they all survived. Will the rainforests survive too? Let's hope so.

Guess what!
More than 25% of the medicines we use come from rainforests.

Comprehension

Answer the questions.

1 What are there in the rainforests?

_____

2 How will the scientists travel?

_____

3 What do companies want to do?

_____

4 Who is Dr Michael Fay?

_____

5 How long did the journey take?

_____

Vocabulary

Complete the sentences with these words.

> arrive   carry   cut down   destroy   survive

1 They haven't got any food or water. How will they _____ ?
2 We mustn't _____ nature.
3 Don't _____ that tree – it's beautiful.
4 When will the famous scientist _____? Tomorrow.
5 This rucksack is very big. I can't _____ it.

Grammar

Future Simple

We use the Future Simple to make predictions about the future. We use **will** with a bare infinitive.
People will cut down the rainforests.

Affirmative

I/you/he/she/it/we/they will (I'll, you'll, he'll, she'll, it'll, we'll, they'll) play

Negative

I/you/he/she/it/we/they will not (won't) play

Question

Will I/you/he/she/it/we/they play?

Short answers

Yes, I/you/he/she/it/we/they will.
No, I/you/he/she/it/we/they won't.

Time expressions

tomorrow, in the morning, this weekend/summer/evening
next week/month/year, in a week/month/year

A Complete the sentences with the correct form of the Future Simple and the verbs in brackets.

1 The scientist _____ (follow) the tornado. ✓

2 We _____ (drive) to the forest. ✗

3 You and I _____ (be) here next week. ✓

4 It _____ (rain) in the evening. ✗

5 There _____ (be) any clouds in the sky. ✗

B Complete the questions about the future with the Future Simple and these verbs. Then write Jim's (short) answers.

be (x2) do drive have live

1 _____ people _____ cars?   _____

2 _____ the weather _____ very hot?   _____

3 _____ we _____ much water?   _____

4 _____ there _____ many trees?   _____

5 _____ some people _____ on the moon? _____

6 _____ robots _____ all the jobs?   _____

Vocabulary

Match.

1 canyon ☐
2 cliff ☐
3 forest ☐
4 mountain ☐
5 ocean ☐
6 waterfall ☐

Listening

🎧 **Listen to the advert and complete the notes.**

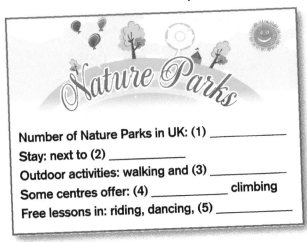

Nature Parks

Number of Nature Parks in UK: (1) _____
Stay: next to (2) _____
Outdoor activities: walking and (3) _____
Some centres offer: (4) _____ climbing
Free lessons in: riding, dancing, (5) _____

🎧 Sounds of English

A Read these pairs of words. What is the difference between the sound of a in each pair? Listen to check.

1 have, save
2 can, danger

B Now put these words in the correct column depending on their a sounds. Listen and check your answers.

black lake map natural nature place

can	save
1 _____	4 _____
2 _____	5 _____
3 _____	6 _____

Looking for TORNADOs!

Read the interview with Brett Jarvis. When do more tornados happen?

Brett Jarvis has an unusual hobby. He likes watching tornados! We asked him about tornados and why he likes them!

Interviewer: What is a tornado?

Brett: A tornado is a very fast and strong wind. It looks like a long black cloud.

Interviewer: Where do you find them?

Brett: There are about 750 tornados a year in the USA. I live in the west of the USA and there are a lot of tornados there. There aren't many mountains so tornados can move very fast.

Interviewer: Are they dangerous?

Brett: Yes! Tornados can lift houses and cars off the ground! They destroy everything near them.

Interviewer: Why do you like getting close to tornados?

Brett: Because it's exciting! When I see a tornado, I follow it in my car and take photographs of it. Sometimes the tornado suddenly comes towards me – that's scary!

Interviewer: What do you do then?

Brett: I drive away from it – fast!

Interviewer: When is the next tornado going to happen in your area?

Brett: Probably very soon. It's May now and there are usually more tornados in spring.

Interviewer: And are you going to follow it?

Brett: Yes, of course! Don't worry, I'll be careful!

Comprehension

Complete the sentences with words from the interview.

1 A tornado looks like a black _____ .

2 There are _____ tornados a year in the USA.

3 Tornados can _____ houses and cars into the air.

4 Brett Jarvis likes taking _____ of tornados.

5 There is a bigger number of tornados in _____ .

Listening

🎧 **Listen and number the pictures in the correct order.**

 a

 d

 b

 e

 c

 f

Speaking

Look at the pictures with your partner and talk about what you think is going to happen. Use these words to help you.

drop	fall off	get wet	run away

Writing

Checking for mistakes

A Always check your work for mistakes in:

punctuation
grammar
spelling
word order

B Tick (✓) the correct sentences and cross (✗) the incorrect ones. Can you correct the mistakes?

1 There are some eagles on that rock? ☐

2 Tornado's are often dangerous. ☐

3 We've got a lot of flowers in our garden. ☐

4 I'm go to visit my cousins this summer. ☐

5 Have you got a umbrella? ☐

6 They'll have a great time in Spain. ☐

C Now read Nigel's letter. Can you find the eight mistakes in the letter?

Dear Juan,

How you are? Are you redy for your trip to England? You'll be here in two weeks!

Ive got lots of plans for your holiday. We going to go cycling in the forest near my house. There's a lake their so we can also go fishing! I'm going take you to a football match too. It be great!

I think the weather will be good in August, sometimes but it rain. Bring a raincoat with you!

See you soon!

Nigel

Task ✏

D Imagine a penfriend is coming to stay with you in your country. Write a letter telling him/her about your plans for their holiday. Use this plan to help you.

Begin like this:
Dear _____,

Paragraph 1
Ask how he/she is.
Ask if he/she is ready for trip.
Say when he/she will be here.

Paragraph 2
Tell him/her your plans for his/her holiday.
Say it will be good/great/fun etc.

Paragraph 3
Tell him/her what the weather will be like.
Tell him/her to bring something with them.

Finish like this:
See you soon!
_____ (your name)

E Read your letter and check your work for mistakes.

Review 6

Vocabulary

A Write the missing letters to make words for animals.

1 It's a small horse.   p _ _ _
2 It is friendly, clever and it lives in the sea.   d _ _ _ _ _ _
3 It's a bird and it can talk!   p _ _ _ _ _
4 It's a baby cat.   k _ _ _ _ _
5 It's green, dangerous and has got very big teeth!   c _ _ _ _ _ _ _ _
6 It's long and thin and it hasn't got any legs.   s _ _ _ _
7 It's like a duck. It's beautiful and has got a long neck.   s _ _ _
8 It's a wild cat. It's big and strong and it's got black spots.   l _ _ _ _ _ _

B Complete the sentences with these words.

> carry   cut down   look for   show   survive   switch on

1 It's dark. _____ the light, please!
2 You can't _____ that box! Give it to me!
3 There aren't any dinosaurs now because they didn't _____ .
4 Can you _____ me the path?
5 We mustn't _____ the trees because a lot of animals live in them.
6 Scientists _____ new kinds of plants and animals in the forest.

C Choose the correct answers.

1 It's very dark inside the _____ .
   a   hill   b   cave   c   cliff
2 I need my umbrella because the weather is _____ .
   a   cloudy   b   windy   c   rainy
3 Be careful! Don't swim near the _____!
   a   rocks   b   path   c   lift
4 Bats are _____ because they sleep in the daytime.
   a   popular   b   important   c   unusual
5 Can you see that eagle in the sky? Use my _____ .
   a   binoculars   b   torch   c   cave

D Find the stickers.

1	2
lift	rainbow

3	4
tornado	medallion

5	6
raincoat	butterfly

7	8
plant	rainforest

Grammar

A The words in bold are wrong. Write the correct words.

1 Dogs are **friendliest** than cats.
_____

2 Summer is the **hotter** season.
_____

3 Mountains are **most** beautiful than cities.
_____

4 Whales are the **big** animals in the world.
_____

5 Bats are uglier **that** butterflies.
_____

6 People are the **more** intelligent animals!
_____

B Complete the sentences with the correct form of **be going to** and these verbs.

| catch | destroy | fall | go | rain | swim |

1 The tree _____ on the car. ✔

2 The elephants _____ in the river. ✗

3 It _____ today. It's sunny. ✗

4 She _____ to bed. ✔

5 They _____ the butterfly. ✗

6 The tornado _____ the house. ✔

C Write short answers.

1 Will it rain tomorrow?

_____

2 Will your mum go shopping at the weekend?

_____

3 Will you and your family go on holiday this summer?

_____

4 Will you have a party on your birthday?

_____

5 Will your teachers give you good marks this year?

_____

Song

Ooh rainy weather, cold windy weather
Rainy weather, windy weather.

It was a dark, cloudy day on a street in London town.
It was windy and cold; then the rain came down.
I didn't have an umbrella, so I went into a shop.
Suddenly I saw her and I started to talk.

'This is really bad weather. Look at me. I got wet.'
She gave me a smile that I will never forget.
The most beautiful, friendly face looked at me.
'Me no talk the good English. Me is French, you see.'

I said 'No, let me tell you what you must say:
I don't speak much English. I am French. OK?'
She didn't like our weather. It was the month of May.
'You have snow, rain, clouds, sun all in one day.'

This is England, I said, and then the rain stopped.
'Do you feel like talking in a coffee shop?'
She said yes, and we sat in a small café
And I became friends with Suzanne that day.

Thank you, rainy weather. You brought us together.
Beautiful Suzanne is my rainbow in the sky.
English weather. Because of you, I met her.
We're going to stay together. We will never say goodbye.

117

The Young Riders of Mongolia

Mongolia
Ulan Bator

Before you watch

A Answer the questions with your partner.

- Do you like horses?
- What do horses look like?
- What do horses eat?

B The story

This story happens near Ulan Bator in Mongolia. Ulan Bator is the capital city of Mongolia.

Words to know

Look at the words and pictures. Find and circle them in the word search.

A	D	E	F	G	R	I	O
M	E	D	A	L	A	D	T
I	Y	L	O	P	C	V	B
L	S	C	E	R	E	N	A
K	W	I	T	F	E	R	S
P	S	T	A	D	I	U	M
C	V	I	I	B	N	E	E
D	T	Y	L	A	R	M	Y

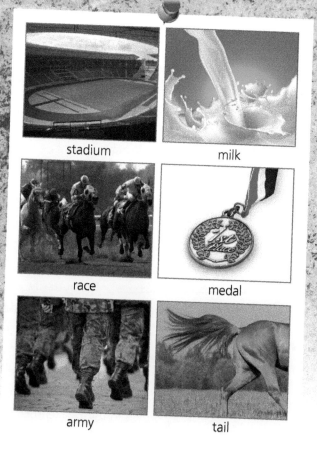

stadium   milk

race   medal

army   tail

While you watch

A Watch the video. Put the sentences in the correct order.

1 The parents and riders walk around a special area. ☐
2 The race ends. ☐
3 The winners ride around the sports ground. ☐
4 The race begins. ☐
5 The winners get medals and horse's milk. ☐
6 The riders prepare for the race. ☐

B Watch again. Circle the words you hear.

1 Every year in May / July, thousands of people come to a place near Ulan Bator.
2 The riders in the race must be less than twelve / ten years old.
3 Before the race the parents / cousins join the young riders to walk around a special area.
4 The people who watch the race want to get near the winning dust / horses.
5 These first riders have already been racing for nearly thirty / thirteen minutes.
6 It's the end of the Nadaam race for another month / year.

After you watch

A Circle the correct answer.

1 Mongolian people are ___ at horse riding.
   a good
   b bad
   c happy
2 There are ___ riders in the race.
   a 1200
   b 500
   c 100

3 The riders in the race are ___ .
   a old
   b young
   c different
4 There is a special ___ at the end of the race.
   a emperor
   b army
   c singer

B Grammar Focus: Fill the gaps with: When, Where, Who, What and Whose.

1 '_____ is the race?' 'July.'
2 '_____ is Genghis Khan?' 'An Emperor.'
3 '_____ is the race?' 'In Ulan Bator, Mongolia.'
4 '_____ do the riders win?' 'Medals and horse's milk.'
5 '_____ horse is this?' 'It's the winner's.'

Project

Plan a festival and make a poster for it. Find or draw and colour the pictures. Tell the class about your festival.

Come to the

Strawberry Festival!

Visit the Strawberry Festival every June!
You can eat yummy strawberries and have fun!!

Don't miss it!
See you there...

Monkey Party

Before you watch

A Answer the questions with your partner.

- Do you like monkeys?
- What do monkeys look like?
- What do monkeys eat?
- Where do monkeys live?

B The story

This story is about monkeys. It happens in Lopburi, Thailand.

Words to know

Match the words to the pictures.

> banquet   cake   festival   monkey   street

_____

_____

_____

_____

_____

While you watch

A Watch the video. Write T (true) or F (false).

1 The monkeys sit on a blue car. ☐
2 People give the monkeys food. ☐
3 There is a lot of fruit on tables. ☐

4 The men are carrying cakes. ☐
5 There is a man wearing red trousers. ☐
6 A monkey eats a yellow flower. ☐

B Watch again. Circle the words you hear.

1 In the town / village of Lopburi, Thailand, monkeys are everywhere.
2 They let the monkeys run around the streets and cause problems / trouble.
3 Most people in Thailand think monkeys are very important animals / heroes.
4 Every day people give food / toys to the monkeys.
5 Every year there are a lot of people who come and help with the monkey festival / banquet.
6 The monkeys don't just like the cake / party, they love it!

After you watch

A Circle the correct answer.

1 Why do the monkeys in Lopburi cause trouble?
   a They get into everything.
   b They are heroes.
   c They eat cake.

2 The monkeys are ___ .
   a worried
   b nice
   c naughty

3 How many times a year do the people have a 'Monkey Party'?
   a 3
   b 2
   c 1

4 ___ people come and help make the cake for the monkey banquet.
   a Fifteen
   b Ten
   c Fifty

B Grammar Focus: Circle the correct answer.

1 There are much / a lot of monkeys in Lopburi.

2 'Is there some / any cake left?' 'Yes, there is.'

3 Much / Many people give food to the monkeys.

4 I've got any / some bananas.

5 I don't want a few / much orange juice.

Project

Write a recipe for a Monkey Party Cake!

Make a cake for the Monkey Party! In groups, make a list of ingredients for the cake.
You need some milk, a lot of butter, etc.

Then draw a picture of your cake and colour it in.

Ingredients

Alaskan Ice Climbing

Before you watch

A **Answer the questions with your partner.**

- Where do you think Alaska is?
- What do you think the weather is like there?
- Would you like to go to Alaska?
- What sports do you think are popular in Alaska?

B **The story**

This story starts in Talkeetna, Alaska, in the United States (U.S.). It ends in an area called Matanuska near Denali National Park.

Alaska
Matanuska

Words to know

A **Match the words to the pictures.**

climbing   hiking   skiing

_____   _____   _____

B **Look at the words and pictures. Find and circle them in the word search.**

G	R	T	O	R	T	E	M	G
C	R	A	M	P	O	N	S	L
R	W	E	O	P	O	C	R	A
E	T	A	S	T	L	H	A	C
V	Y	U	N	K	H	F	I	I
A	S	T	E	B	R	O	E	E
S	H	F	O	G	F	P	R	R
S	K	W	O	T	R	A	I	C
E	S	S	C	L	O	U	D	S

crampons

glacier

crevasse

tool

fog

clouds

While you watch

A Watch the video. Put the sentences in the correct order.

1 Caitlin talks to the visitors. ☐

2 They hike across Matanuska. ☐

3 The climbers meet at the school. ☐

4 They climb the glacier. ☐

5 They put the equipment in the car. ☐

6 They travel to the Matanuska glacier. ☐

B Watch again. Circle the words you hear.

1 They aren't usually worried when they are in the glacier / mountains, but they won't take a small plane out in bad weather.

2 The group get ready to hike / climb part of the Matanuska glacier – a 30-foot wall of ice.

3 The hike across Matanuska is beautiful / easy, but it can also be very dangerous.

4 Seracs are large pieces of blue glacial ice that stick up in the sky / air.

5 It's hard work, but Colby and Caitlin make it look easy / fun.

6 Alaska is home to 100,000 glaciers. These tourists / people can say that they have successfully climbed one – Matanuska.

After you watch

A Circle the correct answer.

1 The climbers want to ___ onto a glacier and ski down it.
   a fly
   b hike
   c climb

2 The Matanuska glacier is ___
   a 200 years old.
   b 2000 years old.
   c 2 years old.

3 The climbers wear ___ on their boots.
   a crampons
   b crevasses
   c tools

4 The climbers feel ___ when they get to the top of the glacier.
   a dangerous
   b bad
   c great

B Grammar Focus: Circle the correct answer.

1 Denali is the higher / highest mountain in North America.

2 Alaska is the larger / largest state in the U.S.A.

3 Alaska is colder / coldest than Spain.

4 Colby and Caitlin are the best / better mountain guides in Talkeetna.

5 Crocodiles are more / most dangerous than parrots.

Project

Read the adverts and choose the trip you like the best. In pairs, talk about why you like it.

Then, think of a holiday you want to go on and make a poster for it.

Amazing Alaska Cruise

Fantastic new ship, delicious meals, sightseeing trips to glaciers and mountains...

Visit Alaska in style!

Mountain Climbing School

Learn how to climb mountains on this two-week course – and see Alaska from the top of Mt. Denali!

Surprise!

Characters

Jake
Kate
Mandy
Robbie
Kate's mum
Kate's dad
Friends

Scene 1

In Kate's living room

It's 11.30 on Saturday morning and Kate is on the phone to Jake.

Kate: Hi, Jake. This is Kate.

Jake: Hi, Kate. How are you?

Kate: I'm bored. How are you?

Jake: I'm fine! Mandy and I are ... erm ... we're finishing our homework now. Then we're ... then we're going skateboarding.

Kate: And what are you doing tonight?

Jake: We're going to the cinema with our parents.

Kate: Oh. Jake, I want to ask you something.

Jake: Sorry, Kate. Mum wants me. See you on Monday. Bye!

Kate: Bye.

Kate feels very sad. Then Robbie comes into the living room.

Robbie: Hello, Kate. I'm looking for my trainers.

Kate: Hi, Robbie.

Robbie: Are you OK?

Kate: No, Robbie. I want to ask you something.

Robbie: Yes?

Kate: What day is it today?

Robbie: It's Saturday 10th May.

Kate: So, you remember!

Robbie: Yes, I remember because I'm going to a friend's party today.

Kate: You're lucky.

Robbie: Yes. It's going to be great!

He finds his trainers behind a chair and starts to walk out of the room.

Robbie: See you, Kate.

Somewhere in the house, Kate's dad is looking for Kate.

Dad: Kate? Kate? Where are you?

Kate: I'm in the living room.

Kate's dad comes into the room.

Dad: What are you doing?

Kate: Nothing. Dad, do you know what day it is?

Dad: It's Saturday today. You always go to Grandma's on Saturdays.

Kate: Yes, but …

Dad: Well, why don't you go and get ready now? I want you to go to Grandma's house at one o'clock. OK?

Kate: OK.

Kate's dad leaves the room.

Kate: But Dad … (*to herself*) It's my birthday today. I'm so sad. No birthday cards, no presents, no friends.

124

Later, at four o'clock, the living room is ready for the party. Everybody is waiting for Kate.

Mandy: Ssh, everybody! She's coming!

Kate comes through the front door of the house.

Kate: Mum? Dad? I'm home.

She comes into the living room.

All: Surprise! Surprise! Happy birthday, Kate!
Robbie: It's a surprise party!
Jake: We played a trick on you!
Mandy: You were so sad this morning, Kate. We're sorry.
Robbie: But we didn't forget your birthday. We invited all your friends.
Dad: We wanted to give you a wonderful surprise.
Kate: It **is** a wonderful surprise, Dad!
Mandy: Kate, here is a present for you.
Robbie: And this is for you, too.
Mum: This is from Dad and me. And here is your birthday cake!
Kate: Thank you very much, everyone! You're all very kind. I will never forget this birthday.
Jake: Let's play some music! Come on everybody.

Scene 2

After Kate leaves the house, her family and friends meet in the living room.

Jake: OK, let's get ready for a big party! I've got the party hats.
Mandy: I've got lots of balloons.
Dad: I'll help you with those, Mandy.
Robbie: Here are Kate's favourite CDs.
Mum: We've also got a lot of her favourite food, and a big birthday cake with candles.
Mandy: This is so exciting! Kate will be very happy.

They get everything ready for the party.

Irregular verbs

Infinitive	Past Simple	Infinitive	Past Simple
be	was/were	light	lit
become	became	make	made
break	broke	meet	met
bring	brought	put	put
buy	bought	read	read [red]
can	could	ride	rode
catch	caught	run	ran
choose	chose	say	said
come	came	see	saw
cost	cost	sell	sold
cut	cut	send	sent
do	did	shine	shone
draw	drew	shoot	shot
drink	drank	sing	sang
eat	ate	sit	sat
fall	fell	sleep	slept
feel	felt	speak	spoke
fly	flew	spend	spent
find	found	stand	stood
forget	forgot	steal	stole
get	got	swim	swam
give	gave	take	took
go	went	teach	taught
have	had	tear	tore
hear	heard	tell	told
hold	held	think	thought
keep	kept	throw	threw
know	knew	understand	understood
learn	learnt	wear	wore
leave	left	win	won
lie	lay	write	wrote

Wonderful World 3 Pupil's Book
Michele Crawford

Publisher: Jason Mann
Director of Content Development: Sarah Bideleux
Commissioning Editor: Carol Goodwright
Development Editor: Lynn Thomson
Assistant Editor: Manuela Barros
Content Project Editor: Amy Smith
Art Director: Natasa Arsenidou
Cover Designer: Vasiliki Christoforidou
Text Designers: Natasa Arsenidou
Compositor: Sophia Ioannidou
National Geographic Editorial Liaison: Leila Hishmeh

Acknowledgements
Illustrated by Theodoros Piakis
Song Credits: Lyrics and music composed
by David Allan
Recorded at Motivation Sound Studios and
GFS-PRO Studio
Production at GFS-PRO Studio by George Flamouridis

The publisher would like to thank the following sources
for permission to reproduce their copyright protected
photos:
Fotolia – p.69 (Sportlibrary); **Istockphoto** – pp. 45 (Ivan
Solis); 81 (Dominik Pabis, Matthew Dixon, Kitchner Bain,
Lee Feldstein, travellinglight), 90–91 (Darko Novakovic);
National Geographic – pp. 18 (MICHAEL S. LEWIS), 28
(LYNN JOHNSON), 36 (BATES LITTLEHALES), 82 (DICK
DURRANCE II), 100 (MICHAEL POLIZA), 108 (MIKE THEISS);
Shutterstock – pp. 13 (Nick Stubbs, David Huntley,
T-Design, Jessie Eldora Robertson, JinYoung Lee), 15 (Jacek
Chabraszewski, Stuart Monk, Kurhan, Rob Marmion,
Losevsky Pavel), 24 (oliveromg, Martin Valigursky), 31
(Monika23, Monkey Business Images, Tomasz Trojanowski,
mashe, Dmitry Melnikov), 33 (Lisa F. Young, AGITA
LEIMANE, Mark Graves, Joel Blit), 42 (Luc Sesselle, Fukuoka
Irina), 43 (Monkey Business Images, Yuri Arcurs), 63
(iofoto , Monkey Business Images), 69 Ljupco Smokovski,
78 (Doug Stacey, Elnur, Bill McKelvie), 85 (photo25th), 95
(Lisa F. Young, Chiyacat, maureen plainfield), 103 (Gelpi,
FloridaStock, clarence s lewis, Pakhnyushcha, Susan
Flashman), 104 (Utekhina Anna, pixel-pets, amattel), 105
(pnicoledolin, Kim Ruoff, Vakhrushev Pavel, N/A, Eric
Isselée, Jiri Vaclavek, Pieter, Monika Wisniewska), 106
(Muellek Josef, sonya etchison, Tracy Whiteside, Linda
Bucklin, Eric Isselée), 107 (javarman, Nataliya Hora,
fivespots, Pichugin Dmitry, Raphael Daniaud), 111 (Dmitry
Yakunin, Doug Baines, Robert Venn, Péter Gudella, Eric
Gevaert), 113 (Sam DCruz, Mana Photo, Willem Dijkstra,
Galyna Andrushko, Mike Norton, yurok), 114 (DarkOne,
Mike VON BERGEN), 121 (Ersler Dmitry); **Thinkstock** –
pp. 13 (Istockphoto), 15 (Jupiterimages), 58 (iStockphoto),
59 (George Doyle/Stockbyte), 63 (iStockphoto), 77
(iStockphoto), 95 (iStockphoto), 106 (iStockphoto).

ISBN: 978-1-111-40217-4

National Geographic Learning
Cheriton House
North Way
Andover
Hampshire
SP10 5BE
United Kingdom

Cengage Learning is a leading provider of customized learning
solutions with office locations around the globe, including
Singapore, the United Kingdom, Australia, Mexico, Brazil and Japan.
Locate your local office at: **international.cengage.com/region**

Cengage Learning products are represented in Canada by
Nelson Education, Ltd.

Visit National Geographic Learning online at **ngl.cengage.com**

Visit our corporate website at **www.cengage.com**

Printed in the United Kingdom by Ashford Colour Press
Print Number 11 Print Year 2019